D1478370

THE BALLAD OF
BEN <u>AND</u>
STELLA MAE

Great Plains Outlaws Who Became
FBI Public Enemies Nos. 1 and 2

Matthew Cecil

University Press of Kansas

Published by the University Press of Kansas (Lawrence, Kansas 66045), which was organized by the Kansas Board of Regents and is operated and funded by Emporia State University, Fort Hays State University, Kansas State University, Pittsburg State University, the University of Kansas, and Wichita State University.

Library of Congress Cataloging-in-Publication Data
Names: Cecil, Matthew, author.
Title: The ballad of Ben and Stella Mae : Great Plains outlaws who became FBI Public Enemies Nos. 1 and 2 / Matthew Cecil.
Description: Lawrence, Kansas : University Press of Kansas, 2016. | Includes bibliographical references and index.
Identifiers: LCCN 2016023590| ISBN 9780700623242 (hardback : alkaline paper) | ISBN 9780700623259 (ebook)
Subjects: LCSH: Dickson, Ben, 1912–1939. | Dickson, Stella Mae, 1922–1995. | Criminals—United States—Biography. | Outlaws—Great Plains—Biography. | Bank robberies—Great Plains—History—20th century. | Kidnapping—Great Plains—History—20th century. | Hoover, J. Edgar (John Edgar), 1895–1972. | United States. Federal Bureau of Investigation—History—20th century. | Great Plains—History—20th century—Biography. | BISAC: TRUE CRIME / General. | HISTORY / United States / 20th Century. | POLITICAL SCIENCE / Political Freedom & Security / Law Enforcement.
Classification: LCC HV6785 .C43 2016 | DDC 364.15/52092278—dc23
LC record available at https://lccn.loc.gov/2016023590.

British Library Cataloguing-in-Publication Data is available.

Printed in the United States of America

10 9 8 7 6 5 4 3 2 1

The paper used in this publication is recycled and contains 30 percent postconsumer waste. It is acid free and meets the minimum requirements of the American National Standard for Permanence of Paper for Printed Library Materials Z39.48-1992.

CONTENTS

CAST OF CHARACTERS

James D. Dickson, Ben's father, taught chemistry at Topeka High School from 1908 until 1943. During World War II, he was a chemist for the Topeka waterworks. He died of a heart attack on January 8, 1959, in his home at 517 W. Fourteenth Street in Topeka. He was eighty-six.

Bertha (Alma) J. Dickson suffered a further mental breakdown after she was told of Ben's death. She rarely left her bedroom and died in 1953, at the age of sixty-five. Bertha and James Dickson are buried in the Dickson family plot in the Auburn (Kansas) Cemetery.

Stella Mae Irwin's stepfather, plasterer **Lester Redenbaugh**, died in 1959. He was sixty-two.

Stella's mother, **Hattie Redenbaugh**, died in 1990, at age eighty-nine.

Stella's brother, **Alvie "Junior" Irwin**, died in 1986, at age sixty-six. Junior, Lester, and Hattie are buried in the Rochester Cemetery, in Topeka.

James Darwin Dickson, Ben's brother, worked forty-five years for the Santa Fe Railway. He and his first wife, Frances Bonnell, had one son, James Darwin Dickson, Jr., in 1929. James Darwin Dickson, Jr., lives in Citrus Heights, California. Darwin and his second wife, Fanchion Pitman, had two sons, John and Richard. John is retired and lives in Chanute, Kansas. Richard is an attorney and practices in Wichita. Darwin Dickson died on July 14, 1999, in Colony, Kansas, at the age of ninety-one. He is buried in the Colony Cemetery.

PREFACE

After searching for years, I located Stella Mae Irwin in 1996, about a year after her death. According to Stella's family members, it is just as well that I never found her in life. When I suggested to Stella's great-nieces Renee Araiza and Gloria Seematter and their father, Richard Araiza, that had I knocked on her door Stella probably would have told me to "Go to hell," they laughed and agreed that was highly likely. Their stern but loving aunt never spoke about her secret past as a public enemy with anyone. Stella's mementos of 1938 and 1939 sat in boxes in a storage shed at her home in the Kansas City neighborhood of Raytown, Missouri, locked away and hidden from everyone, including her family. We have only a hint of what those boxes may have contained. A neighbor who inherited Stella's belongings once sent me a series of color copies of photographs of Stella and her husband, Ben, copies of some of which I obtained separately from the Dickson family. There were images of Stella and Ben at the Topeka Free Fair in 1938, posing in novelty "Tiajuana" scenes. There was a colorized photograph of Ben taken in San Francisco that year. Those copied photographs provided me with my first glimpse of Ben and Stella as human beings rather than as the manufactured public enemies of Federal Bureau of Investigation (FBI) lore.

My interest in the FBI portion of the Ben and Stella story dates back to my teen years in my hometown, Brookings, South Dakota. Ben and Stella robbed the Northwest Security National Bank there on Halloween in 1938. Brookings bills itself as "someplace special," and to me that could not be more true. My earliest memories are of visiting my father at his office on the South Dakota State University campus in Brookings and of attending Jackrabbit football games with him on glorious fall afternoons (and a few snowy ones, too.) As a teenager I began working as a dishwasher in a Main Avenue restaurant, The Ram Pub, located in a building that once housed the Northwest Security National Bank. A freestanding, round pedestal safe still stands in the back of the restaurant and was likely the safe opened by John Torsey on that day in 1938 when Ben Dickson, accompanied by his sixteen-year-old wife, Stella, robbed the bank. Perhaps because the restaurant there still celebrates and identifies with the robbery and perhaps also because major crime is so rare in Brookings, those two hours during which the Dicksons waited for the bank vault's time lock to open remain among the most infamous 120 minutes in the city's history. The robbery captured my imagination as I spent slow times at the restaurant reading and rereading the framed news clippings on the wall and imagining events that happened just a few feet from where I stood. Right there in the back of the restaurant was where Ben ordered Torsey to open the safe and empty the $2,000 it contained into a pillow sack while they waited for the vault to open. There, near the entrance of the restaurant, was where Stella Mae stood guard, awkwardly wielding a revolver wrapped in a newspaper. Over near the front of the restaurant was where Ben sat while the bank's manager processed several loans during the robbery. The front door of the restaurant, which I passed through thousands of times, is where Ben poked a sawed-off shotgun in Torsey's back and forced his way into the bank. My imaginary time travel was sparked by myriad details in the bank and dozens of other details around Brookings. Many times I drove home from work following the route Ben and Stella took after the robbery, passing the old boardinghouse near the Brookings County Courthouse where they dropped off their hostages. I stood at the corner of Sixth Street and Medary and watched the Hobo Day homecoming parade of South Dakota State University (SDSU) pass by, imagining the Dicksons' lumbering black Buick making the turn north onto Medary Avenue, Stella tossing roofing nails out of the car to discourage pursuers. A combination gas station and restaurant near Hillcrest Park marked the location of the Macomb Gas Station where Ben and Stella stopped briefly on their way out of town so Ben could be sure the nails hadn't punctured his tires. The horseshoe pits in Hillcrest Park, where I played often as a child, marked the location of the rustic City Cabin Camp, where Ben and Stella stayed before the robbery.

My fascination with the Dicksons was something I kept private for many years before I obtained their FBI files. This slim volume, the best story I can tell about the Dicksons based on existing records, is a work of passion and fascination decades in the making. It is the kind of book that would not be possible without the help of many people. Wichita State University colleagues Jessica Freeman, Kevin Keplar, Bill Molash, Sandy Sipes, and Amy Solano provided endless good humor that lightened my writing hours in the office. I am grateful to officials in the Records Management Division of the FBI, who respond each year to tens of thousands of Freedom of Information Act (FOIA) requests, including the hundreds I have filed over the past two decades. Rebecca Bronson and David P. Sobonya are the names I know from that unit who have been particularly helpful, but obviously there are many others, and I am grateful to them all. The FBI's Freedom of Information and Privacy Act staff has always been responsive to me and, while there have been a few disputes, I am certain that they have done their best within the limits of the law to provide me with the information I have requested.

Similarly, the FOIA staff of the Bureau of Prisons and the Department of Justice responded quickly and professionally to my requests related to the Dicksons. The National Archives and Records Administration staff was helpful as well during a fruitful visit to College Park, Maryland. Archivists at the Kansas State Historical Society in Topeka, the State Historical Society of Missouri in Jefferson City, and the South Dakota Historical Society in Pierre also provided timely research assistance. Michele Christian and the staff at H. M. Briggs Library Special Collections at SDSU provided photographs from the extraordinary George and Evelyn Norby Collection of local historical photos. The reference staff at the Missouri State Archives provided copies of Ben Dickson's 1931 admission mug shot and prison ledger entry. I am grateful as well to Editor-in-Chief Michael Briggs, Director

Charles T. Myers, and the staff at the University Press of Kansas for designing, marketing, and, of course, agreeing to publish the book. This is my third book published by the University Press of Kansas, and I am as grateful for their confidence in me as I am for their able help in preparing this book and the two others, *Hoover's FBI and the Fourth Estate* (2014) and *Branding Hoover's FBI* (2016).

Several people who knew Ben and Stella provided help, even though, in some instances, it was painful or uncomfortable for them. Ben's older brother Darwin Dickson spoke to me twice on the telephone in 1995 for about an hour each time. Recalling his brother, whom he referred to as "the little guy," was emotional for him and I am grateful for his help. Darwin died in 1999 at age ninety-one. Sharon Michael, Stella's neighbor for decades, twice spoke to me in 1999, fondly remembering her friend. Repeated attempts to recontact Michael in 2015 proved fruitless. Mary Ellen Dickson, whose husband is a second cousin to Ben, graciously provided pages from a family history authored by Darwin Dickson.

Gloria (Araiza) Seematter, Renee Araiza, and Richard Araiza spoke lovingly of their Aunt and Great-Aunt Stella and provided several of the photographs in this volume. Their stories helped bring Stella to life, and to their concerns that they might be betraying their beloved aunt's privacy by speaking, I can only respond that Stella's story of survival is one that inspires me and that I hope inspires readers. Ben Dickson's nephews John Dickson, of Chanute, Kansas, and Richard Dickson, of Wichita, were also extremely helpful. Richard Dickson, a Wichita attorney, entrusted me with a massive trunk full of precious family photographs saved by his father, Darwin. The Dickson family photographs constitute the majority of the images in this book.

There is one other historian who was immensely helpful, someone who knows more about the history of Brookings than anyone else I know, my father, Chuck Cecil. Dad answered my questions about obscure Brookings-area landmarks as if those sites—the City Tourist Camp, Macomb's, the Tasty Shop—still stood. Of course, help with a short book is the least of the things my parents have done for me.

For all of their help, I am eternally grateful. The finished draft manuscript was read by my wonderful WSU colleague Sandy Sipes, and I am grateful for her encouragement and skillful editing. Finally, the inspiration for this book came from the prodding of my wife, Jen, and son, Owen. Owen in particular urged me to write this story, reasoning that since I know more about the Dicksons' exploits than anyone else alive, it would be a shame if their story wasn't published. Well, Owen, here it is.

THE BALLAD OF
BEN AND
STELLA MAE

INTRODUCTION

Beyond this place of wrath and tears
Looms but the Horror of the shade,
And yet the menace of the years
Finds and shall find me unafraid.
—*from "Invictus," by William Ernest Henley,*
Ben Dickson's favorite poem

The case of married bank robbers and Public Enemies Ben and Stella
Mae Dickson generated news coverage nationwide from late 1938 into
mid-1939. Newspapers from coast to coast, prompted by FBI news
releases, speculated about the fugitive bank robbers' locations, retold
embellished versions of their exploits, and trumpeted Ben Dickson's
death when he was shot by an FBI agent on a South Euclid Avenue
sidewalk in St. Louis. The Dicksons' story contains all the elements of
a Hollywood motion picture: romance, action, and tragedy. Ben Dickson was a handsome, charismatic young man. Stella Mae Dickson was
a pretty, blonde young woman. While Ben and Stella Mae Dickson

have never achieved the notoriety of famed 1930s outlaws like John Dillinger or Bonnie Parker and Clyde Barrow, their story remains a regional favorite in Kansas and South Dakota. Newspaper reports about the Dicksons have appeared as recently as 2014 in Topeka. Topeka law enforcement historian Joe Zimmer kept the story alive in Kansas for decades after many people had forgotten. The Dicksons' story is perpetuated in Brookings, South Dakota, by owners of the restaurant that now occupies the bank building they robbed there in 1938. For several years recently, downtown Brookings also hosted an annual "Robbery Days" street sale in the summer wherein Main Avenue merchants offered "crazy" deals, bouncy castles, and dunk tanks alongside robbery reenactments in an event promoted by local businesses in the same sensational way J. Edgar Hoover's FBI sold its pursuit of the Dicksons in 1938 and 1939.

Unfortunately for Ben and Stella Mae Dickson, they came along at a time when Hoover's FBI was perfecting its public relations machinery and honing its facile message of good versus evil. It was also a time when newspaper reporters and editors routinely restated and even embellished the characterizations of the Bureau's designated public enemies, as provided by Hoover's publicists. Ben and Stella emerged from Topeka, Kansas, as small-time outlaws at a time when Hoover and his publicists needed public enemies to act as easily defeated foils in the Bureau's self-promotion campaigns. Dillinger and the other famed bandits were long gone by 1939, but the media's appetite for Bureau adventures had to be sated. Historians have suggested that the FBI chose for decades to focus on its work in relatively simple criminal cases rather than admit the existence, for example, of a complex criminal mafia or La Cosa Nostra in America. In contrast to the complex task of untangling organized crime families bonded by a vow of silence, dramatic outlaw cases required time-consuming but elementary police work, readily captured the public's attention, and generated enormous outpourings of support for the Bureau whenever a public enemy was captured or killed.

Journalism is sometimes referred to as the first draft of history. In the case of the Dicksons, it is a poor and inaccurate draft, one that emphasizes caricature over truth and twists facts to fit the simplified narrative template of good versus evil promoted by Hoover and his public relations team. The public enemies of the 1930s were not uniformly evil. Some, of course, were more violent and dangerous than others, but there was no room for nuance of that sort in the Bureau's publicity campaigns. Instead, the worst of the outlaws, like deranged murderers Bonnie and Clyde and charismatic bank robber and killer Dillinger, defined the rest, no matter the facts. In its press releases on the Dickson case, for example, the FBI plainly stated that none of the criminals the Bureau sought "was more vicious than Benjamin James [sic] Dickson."[1] Playing off of that claim, *True* magazine published a story in 1939 about the Dicksons headlined "The Crimson Trail of Public Enemies One and Two," stating, "You and your neighbors are in danger while they roam the country, robbing and terrorizing."[2] Instead of complexity, stories of public enemies were peddled by the FBI like cornflakes using a simple marketing formula that defined all criminals worthy of the Bureau's attention as equally depraved and threatening to the American way of life. The dramatic tales of FBI exploits, with moral and highly trained agents employing science in the quest to bring murderous public enemies to justice, became surefire hits among a Depression-era public desperate for evidence that surely some institution in America's broken society still worked.

In 1939, even as Hoover secretly worked to expand the FBI's jurisdiction to include spying on dissenting Americans, public interest in the Dicksons provided the Bureau with the opportunity to recycle the myth of the infallible G-Men, the faceless, highly trained, omnipresent foot soldiers seeking and neutralizing public enemies. Throughout the 1930s, the Bureau hyped its public enemies as merely the most visible of criminals who were hiding in plain sight. Outlaws like Ben Dickson, in the FBI's narratives, emerged even from middle-class neighborhoods as immoral nihilists determined to destroy the country. Scholars have repeatedly demonstrated that media representations, particularly those of criminals, are artificial constructions, based on facts provided by law enforcement but ultimately subject to simplification and distortion as journalists sort criminals into a set of well-understood and accepted categories. Hoover and his public relations team recognized that tendency and also came to understand that journalists in the 1930s were willing to "join the team" and cheer the Bureau's exploits. Journalists became adjunct members of the FBI public relations team, even to the point of exaggerating the already distorted versions of events and twisted representations of individual criminals provided by Bureau publicists.[3] The public loved those sorts of FBI hosannas, and the Bureau's exploits were popular with the public precisely because of the compelling and dramatic way they were presented in the news and entertainment media.

Readers, viewers, and listeners came to expect stories of outlaws who were "good boys gone wrong" and their women companions, who were either vicious gun molls or immoral trollops, or some combination of the two. Hoover's publicists happily fulfilled those expectations. With readers and listeners conditioned to accept and always prepared to celebrate the Bureau's law enforcement successes, Hoover was free to secretly expand the work of his FBI into domestic spying while Americans were distracted by tales of outlaws, foreign spies, and subversive Communists. The FBI's law enforcement successes, shaped into dramatic narratives by Bureau publicists and friendly journalists, were inarguably successful in molding public perceptions of Hoover and his G-Men. To the American public, the FBI of 1938 and 1939 was a responsible, scientific, law enforcement agency, and an indispensable one at that. Criminals like Ben and Stella Mae Dickson, on the other hand, were, to use a term Hoover often favored, "vermin" to be exterminated on sight.

Historical narrative is, of course, also a simplification, but one based on a much broader historical context and a more complete set of facts. In the case of Hoover's FBI, facts are readily available. The director's information-gathering and indexing skills, honed during his first federal government job at the Library of Congress, were operationalized in the FBI. As a result, the Bureau has left behind vast stores of historical

J. Edgar Hoover, pictured here on April 5, 1940, served as Director of the FBI from 1924 until his death on May 2, 1972. (Courtesy of the Library of Congress, Harris & Ewing Collection, Call Number LC-H22-D-8744.)

evidence that are available for review via the Freedom of Information Act. That information-gathering and indexing skill is an unappreciated part of the Bureau's long-term success. Part of what made Hoover's FBI effective at weaving together the patchwork of local law enforcement in the 1930s was its remarkable ability to gather, hold, and analyze vast stores of information, finding patterns or linking people and events across jurisdictional boundaries. The serial number on an automobile engine located by local police in a garage in St. Joseph, Missouri, suddenly had the potential to help solve a bank robbery in Elkton, South Dakota, because the FBI gathered and held that information centrally. The typewriter used to type a ransom note could potentially be traced and identified. Hoover's early embrace of fingerprint science in the 1920s, when most American law enforcement agencies rejected it as unproven alchemy, meant that a partial fingerprint found at a crime scene in Texas or Oklahoma could identify a criminal from New York or Delaware as the culprit.

Because the Bureau was so thorough in its information gathering and record keeping, Hoover's secret files hold a treasure trove of information. In the days before ubiquitous and instantaneous information-sharing networks, local police were hampered by their lack of communication with other far-flung law enforcement agencies. With no "local" jurisdictional lines to worry about, the FBI's massive cache of information oftentimes had significant evidentiary value, and thousands of crimes were solved because the Bureau could find and analyze the kind of minutiae that might have been lost or overlooked by local law enforcement. While the Bureau's crime laboratory has often garnered a majority of the public imagination and is credited with many of the FBI's investigative successes, the reality is that simple information gathering, indexing, and analysis were among the FBI's most important contributions to law enforcement.

The Bureau's fetish for collecting and holding data, of course, has also been a boon to historians. After Hoover's death in 1972, the wraps began to come off the "secret" files of the FBI. Expansions of the Freedom of Information Act in the mid-1970s further opened Hoover's files to researchers, and revelations of the FBI's excessive and sometimes illegal investigations have continued to emerge for four decades. Even more information has become available as historians have gradually decoded Hoover's filing system, mining the arcane markings on files to identify and request new files. Every FBI file is a puzzle piece, including potential clues to filling out a larger picture by identifying and obtaining other relevant files from among the massive cache of information held by the Bureau. Today, tens of thousands of the millions of dossiers compiled by the FBI on cases, people, organizations, and social movements are part of the public record.

In the mid-1990s, the FBI file no. 7-2561, on Ben and Stella Mae

Dickson, some 4,716 pages of it, was released to the author of this book. The "7" in the file index number indicates that the topic of the file is kidnapping. Despite ostensibly covering only their 1938 kidnapping of three men in Michigan, the Dicksons' 7 file contains extensive coverage of their entire year as fugitives, along with detailed accounts of the Bureau's investigation of the bank robberies they committed. Other files on the Dicksons, from the FBI, the Department of Justice, and the Bureau of Prisons, have followed as the author and others have traced the trail of information. In some cases, the information trail was circumvented by dubious loopholes in the Freedom of Information Act, such as when the FBI was allowed to destroy its files specific to the Dicksons' bank robberies in Elkton and Brookings, South Dakota. Still, this manuscript is based on the review of perhaps fifteen thousand pages of federal government documents and an additional several thousand pages of newspaper accounts supplemented by a handful of interviews with those who remain alive decades after Ben Dickson was killed and Stella Mae Dickson (née Irwin) quietly disappeared into obscurity in Kansas City in the early 1960s.

Those documents and interviews provide a more complex, nuanced view of the case of Ben and Stella Mae Dickson and of the people involved than do the simplistic and stereotypical caricatures of newspapers, FBI, and later book, radio, and even comic book accounts of their exploits. The FBI's public relations releases about the Dicksons, repeated and sometimes embellished by journalists, left behind a popular judgment of Ben and Stella that was unequivocal. They were vicious and immoral criminals prone to violence. The erroneous implication of those portrayals was that it was merely luck, and not their own moral code, that kept Ben and Stella from emulating the murderous violence of Bonnie and Clyde.

This book attempts to flesh out the stories of their lives, adding detail from internal FBI and other government documents, revisiting previous conclusions, and, in the process, perhaps restoring some of each person's individual complexity and humanity. The FBI's fanciful story of Ben and Stella Mae Dickson told of a Bonnie and Clyde–style couple, rudderless and immoral, on a violent rampage across the country. They were vicious and lawless outcasts bent on creating chaos. According to FBI publicists, Ben was the good boy gone wrong, a Kansas version of Clyde Barrow apparently willing to shoot it out with authorities (although he never did) at any moment. Stella was the similarly ruthless and immoral Bonnie Parker–style gun moll, dangerous, unpredictable, and violent. The truth is there is no comparison between the two couples. Ben and Stella were small-time criminals who, while they no doubt did frighten innocent people and take money and automobiles that were not theirs, did not physically harm anyone during their bank robberies or subsequent six months as fugitive public enemies.

Thanks to the meticulous record keepers in Hoover's FBI, we can finally, nearly eight decades later, replace those sensational and oversimplified media caricatures of Ben and Stella with the following story of two flawed, complicated young people from Topeka who became J. Edgar Hoover's Public Enemies No. 1 and No. 2 in 1938. This book offers in place of the depraved outlaw of FBI lore a misguided Ben Dickson who repeatedly made poor choices or let his temper get the better of him. Ben justified his actions based on a combination of feeling he had been treated unjustly by Topeka authorities as a teenager and a promise to use his new start to do good and make his father proud of him again. More poignantly, the book reconsiders "gun moll" Stella Mae Dickson by highlighting the many tragedies of her life, among them the influence of Ben, that transformed her from an ebullient teenager at a Topeka roller rink into a sometime recluse hidden away behind the walls of her Kansas City home.

1

STELLA

Arthur G. Hoffman felt there was something strange about the sullen young woman who sat fidgeting nervously in the backseat of his Buick. The young woman, just sixteen years old, told Hoffman her destination was Topeka, Kansas. She told Hoffman she planned to make arrangements there for a funeral. Hoffman noticed that the young woman was upset, could not sit still, and clung too tightly to her purse. When Hoffman first saw her on the morning of April 7, 1939, at the Mike Longo Travel Bureau in downtown St. Louis, she jumped from a taxi cab, stormed into the office, and interrupted Hoffman's conversation with the proprietor to request a ride to Kansas City. During the first half of the twentieth century, travel bureaus, where people could meet to share long-distance rides, were commonplace. The young woman asked Longo if any cars were going to Kansas City and how much the trip would cost. Longo told her that Hoffman was taking passengers that evening for a three-dollar fare.[1]

The frazzled and emotionally drained young woman was Stella Mae Dickson.[2] She was slim, pretty, about 5 feet 2 inches tall, and her hair was dyed an inconsistent, sandy brown to hide its distinctive blonde color. Her normal tidy and stylish countenance gave way that morning to the disheveled look of someone who had spent the night hiding in the backseat of a car parked in a rented garage. A Topeka native, Stella grew up in difficult circumstances. Her birth father, Alvie A. Irwin, allegedly abused his family and disappeared from their lives almost completely after a divorce when Stella was two years old. Stella's mother, Alta, known as Hattie, was married three times. Her first marriage, to Raymond Baldwin, lasted only a few months and produced one daughter, Virginia, born in 1917. Hattie then married Irwin, a sometimes employed truck driver, and they had two children, Alvie, Jr., born in 1920, and Stella, born two years later. Virginia left home before Stella's misadventures began. Three years after Hattie divorced Irwin, she married a more stable man, a plasterer and laborer named Lester Redenbaugh. Redenbaugh was, by all accounts, a good provider and was kind to his new family.

Like many families during the Great Depression, the Redenbaughs fell on hard times in the mid-1930s. According to social workers' reports, the family lived in a small home at 2401 Southwest Clay Street in a "rather poor part" of Topeka, the capital city of Kansas. Located about sixty miles west of Kansas City, Missouri, Topeka was founded in 1854 and incorporated in 1859. In 1861, when Kansas joined the union, Topeka was chosen as the state capital. With a population of more than sixty thousand in the 1930s, Topeka was the third most populous city in the state, trailing only the Kansas portion of Kansas City and the state's largest city, Wichita. During the Great Depression, a combination of poverty, crime, and an increased urban population transformed what had been comfortable, working-class neighborhoods, like the one the Redenbaughs lived in, into somewhat rougher, unkempt versions of themselves.[3]

Stella later reported that while her stepfather was a hard worker and good provider, the two were not close. Hattie was described in social workers' reports as an attractive woman and "interesting conversationalist" who was self-centered and always maintained an emotional

Stella Mae Irwin was born in Topeka in 1922. She is pictured here in 1923 with her mother Hattie and and older brother Alvin, known in the family as Junior. (Photo courtesy Gloria Seematter, from the Araiza family collection.)

distance from Stella, never fully committing to parenting her daughter in those early years. Their close relationship later in life raises questions about that judgment. If Hattie was distant, it may have been because Stella's older brother, Alvie, known within the family as Junior, contracted infantile paralysis as a young child, perhaps leaving Hattie preoccupied with his care, particularly during the years before her remarriage, when she was responsible for her three children on her own. Junior was disabled by his illness and was unable to work for the rest of his life.

Later in life, Stella and her mother were quite close. Stella was, by all accounts, a typical teen in that she could be moody and angry and, according to her mother, "fought at the drop of a hat." She was, however, a good student in school, scoring As and Bs in most subjects. According to her ninth-grade principal, Stella "was never a bad influence in school and was not a disciplinary problem at all." In contrast to that rosy assessment, two years later, after a string of tragedies and misadventures, Stella was described by those responsible for her care as a young woman "thirsty for affection and attention" who "seems to appreciate friendliness but does not know how to be friendly."

The first tragedy to befall Stella was surely the most horrific. On Halloween night, 1937, Stella and her friend Mary Robinson were walking home from a Topeka roller-skating rink. Roller-skating rinks were a popular small-town recreation and, more importantly for teenagers, they were social gathering places. That night as they walked home from the roller-skating rink, a man stopped to offer the two young women a ride. In the dark, the two girls thought they recognized the driver as a Topeka High School boy, but when they got in the car, they realized he was a stranger, about thirty years old. The man dropped Mary at her home, and then instead of taking Stella home, he drove "as fast as he could" to a spot outside of Topeka and attempted to seduce her. Stella had just turned fifteen two months earlier and told the man she "had not yet gone with boys." She continued to rebuff his advances, and after Stella slapped him the man became violent and attacked her, knocking her unconscious. When Stella regained consciousness, she

Lester and Hattie Redenbaugh, circa 1940s. (Photo courtesy of Gloria Seematter, from the Araiza family collection.)

told prison case workers two years later, she was being raped. After the attack, the man drove Stella back to the Topeka city limits and let her out of the car. Dazed and seriously injured, Stella walked to her mother's house near Washburn College, arriving after two o'clock in the morning. Her injuries were so severe that she was bedridden for two weeks. In late November, when Stella confided in her mother that she had been raped, Hattie Redenbaugh arranged for her daughter to be examined at the Topeka Municipal Clinic, where she was found to have contracted gonorrhea from the attacker.[4]

Gonorrhea is a bacterial infection, sometimes called "the clap," that can lead to serious complications if left untreated. Today, treatment for gonorrhea involves administering powerful antibiotics that eliminate the infection in a few days. As a result, the chronic form of the infection is now relatively uncommon. In the preantibiotic era, however, treatments for gonorrhea were harsh, invasive, and painful. Most treatments employed Mercurochrome, a toxic disinfectant containing poisonous mercury, to kill the bacteria. The most common treatment in the 1930s involved a regimen in which a 1- to 5-percent Mercurochrome solution was repeatedly applied to the vagina and cervix and introduced via a catheter into the urethra every day for weeks until three consecutive cultures for the bacteria that causes gonorrhea came up negative. In addition to being uncomfortable, vaginal and catheter Mercurochrome treatments sometimes resulted in searing pain and significant injury. Another common treatment regimen employed intravenous Mercurochrome treatments. Under the intravenous regimen, a 1-percent Mercurochrome solution, again with toxic mercury as a main ingredient, was administered, with the total volume determined by the patient's weight. Heat exposure was also found to kill the bacteria that caused gonorrhea. Heat treatments involved the insertion of vaginal and rectal probes that were heated to as much as 111 degrees for up to four hours. Often, the Mercurochrome and heat treatments were administered together for weeks. Combined with regular pelvic examinations and cultures, the treatments for gonorrhea that Stella likely endured were painful, invasive, toxic, and dehumanizing. Only fifteen at the time, Stella was no doubt doubly traumatized when, after being raped by a stranger, the treatments for her resulting condition turned out to be brutal, long-term, and dehumanizing. Today, in addition to antibiotic treatment, a rape victim who contracted a sexually transmitted disease would undoubtedly be offered professional counseling and support to help heal the emotional wounds that linger after such an attack.[5] The available records indicate that Stella received no offer of counseling. Her rape and gonorrhea were treated medically, and if she received any counseling, it was provided by her mother.

After about thirty treatments at the municipal clinic, fifteen-year-old Stella refused to continue. Two years later, a case worker reported, "Subject says that it was so embarrassing for her to take these treatments, that she became defiant, uncooperative and did not realize that they were curing her of this dreadful disease." The public health system in the 1930s, however, was not set up to address that sort of understandably defiant response from a teenager. Stella's refusal to continue treatment resulted in a referral to Shawnee County Juvenile Court and, when she continued to refuse treatment, a Shawnee County public health official issued an order remanding her to the State Industrial School in Lansing, Kansas.

The chief probation officer for the Shawnee County Juvenile Court later described Stella as "always very resentful" and "very sullen." That lack of sympathy for a fifteen-year-old rape victim was typical of the evaluations she received then and eighteen months later, when she was a seventeen-year-old convicted felon. There seemed to be no understanding, even among counselors and psychologists, of the feelings of guilt and shame a young woman might experience as the result of a violent sexual assault or of the impact those feelings might have on a teenager's emotional well-being. The shame Stella experienced became public when word of her rape and diagnosis of gonorrhea leaked out to the community. Stella's embarrassing and, in the 1930s, stigmatizing situation soon became well known among her friends and neighbors. According to a 1943 report by her prison case worker, "She felt the disgrace when health officers failed to keep her story secret.

The shame of having her schoolmates and friends know of [the rape] and her subsequent treatments made her bitter and resistive." Even today, public judgments of people with sexually transmitted diseases can be harsh and unsympathetic. In 1938, a young rape victim like Stella would likely have been ostracized, shunned, and shamed, as her friends and neighbors whispered and speculated about the true nature of her plight. On April 18, 1938, to escape the public shame and to avoid being sent to the Kansas State Industrial School, Stella stole a thirty-five-dollar check from her mother, boarded a bus at the Topeka bus station, and ran away to California. Just fifteen years old, Stella would be on her own, separated from her family support system for the next several months.

Sometime after the Halloween 1937 attack, Stella's friend Mary Robinson and her family had moved to Stockton, California, located about eighty-five miles east of San Francisco. After she ran away, Stella stayed with the Robinsons for several days. At some point after she arrived in California, Stella reconnected with an older man named Johnny O'Malley, whom she had met the previous year. Johnny O'Malley was an alias used by fellow Topeka native Ben Dickson. The two had planned to meet when she arrived, she later claimed. According to one version of the story Stella told authorities, Ben had traveled from his home in Los Angeles to stay at a tourist camp in Stockton so they could meet. Other records indicate that their rendezvous was unplanned and that Ben sent Stella a telegram from Stockton asking her to come to visit. While the meeting itself may or may not have been planned, the timing of the meeting appears to have been improvised. In a letter to "Johnny" dated April 13, 1938, just five days before she left Kansas, Stella wrote that she had only "6 more weeks of school," which suggests that her departure, five days later, was a spur-of-the-moment decision. Still another report, a 1939 prison counselor's report, says that Ben was dating Mary Robinson when Stella arrived and that it was only when they broke up that he and Stella got together. The prison report, issued as it was after events had played out and during an interview when she told the story of being raped, seems the most reliable.

Whatever the circumstances of their rendezvous, Stella later found out that Johnny O'Malley's real name was Ben Dickson. Their meeting in California was the beginning of a tumultuous year that would end in Ben's violent death and Stella's imprisonment.

Just under twelve months after running away and connecting with Ben in Stockton, Stella was alone in St. Louis trying to get home to her mother in Topeka. At about 4:30 p.m. on April 7, 1939, Stella returned to the Mike Longo Travel Bureau in St. Louis to meet Hoffman for her ride to Kansas City. Hoffman noticed immediately that the young woman was even more unsettled than she had been that morning. He also noticed that, unlike someone planning to travel hundreds of miles, she carried no luggage. Stella paced nervously back and forth across the travel bureau office, her actions so unnerving that Longo asked Hoffman to take her to a nearby lunch stand for a cup of coffee while they waited for a second passenger to arrive. At 6:00 p.m., the trio set off for Kansas City with Hoffman driving, the unnamed second passenger in the front seat, and Stella in the backseat of the lumbering late-1930s Buick four-door sedan.

Soon after they departed, Stella asked Hoffman to stop because she felt ill. After a brief stop at a service station, she returned to the car, and for the remainder of the 250-mile trip Stella offered only spare conversation in response to Hoffman's questions. The strange nature of her disjointed responses and non sequiturs further disturbed Hoffman. Stella told Hoffman that "they" had a new Buick Century similar to his car. When Hoffman asked, she said "they" referred to herself and her husband. She told Hoffman about a car wreck in which she and her husband rolled their Buick while traveling 105 miles per hour near Osage City, Kansas, south of Topeka, adding that neither they nor their friends were injured in the crash. In response to Hoffman's questions, Stella said that her name was Frances Cameron and that she had family in Topeka, friends in Stockton, California, and an uncle in St. Louis. Hoffman thought it odd when, unprompted, she mentioned newspaper stories that had appeared that afternoon reporting the indictment of Kansas City Democratic political boss Tom Pendergast

Stella Mae Redenbaugh at the home she and Ben Dickson rented in Los Angeles in 1938. (Photo courtesy of Richard L. Dickson, from the Dickson family collection.)

on tax evasion charges. According to Hoffman, the young woman specifically mentioned her disdain for the paid informants of the Federal Bureau of Investigation (FBI) who helped the Bureau make the case against Pendergast. Stella also told Hoffman that the "God damned woman in red" who had lured John Dillinger into an FBI trap in 1934 "should have been killed." Even that sort of implied criticism of the FBI was unusual in the late 1930s. At one point, Hoffman, skeptical about her stories and confused by the odd conversation, asked her to tell him the truth. Stella said, without elaborating, that she was going to Topeka to make arrangements for a funeral. She became so distraught at that point that Hoffman later told authorities that he feared she would commit suicide. "I wanted to ditch her as soon as possible," he later told the FBI.

The car reached Kansas City a few minutes after midnight on April 8, 1939, and Hoffman dropped his front seat passenger off at a private home on Concordia Street. He drove Stella to downtown Kansas City and asked her where she wanted to stay the night. Hoffman stopped at the Congress Hotel, located at the corner of Cherry and East Ninth Streets in downtown Kansas City, and urged her to book a room there, but the panicked young woman refused to leave the car. She began acting even more strangely and told Hoffman that if they were arrested he should tell authorities they were married. Stella then asked him to drive her outside the city to find a spot where they could sleep safely in the car. Fearing that if he dropped her off she would kill herself, Hoffman drove to a secluded spot and slept in the front seat with Stella in the back. They awakened at about 7:30 a.m. on Saturday, April 8, and Stella immediately asked him to drive her to Topeka.

Hoffman was an experienced travel bureau driver. He made his living ferrying passengers from his home in Los Angeles to Kansas City and between Kansas City and St. Louis. Thousands of Americans were on the road during the Great Depression searching for opportunity, often paying a few dollars to travel in private cars rather than take more expensive trains or buses. Hoffman was accustomed to shuttling people from town to town, and it was not unusual, he told FBI agents, for some of those passengers to behave strangely. The young woman in his car that morning stood out as particularly odd. She seemed depressed, carried no luggage, refused to sleep in a hotel, and asked him to tell authorities who might confront them that she was his wife. Hoffman came to believe that she was in serious trouble. "I made up my mind to get rid of her," he later told the FBI. When she again asked him to take her to Topeka, Hoffman said he could not do it and took the opportunity to drop her off at a bus station at the corner of Tenth and McGee Streets in downtown Kansas City. When she refused to leave the car, Hoffman lied and told Stella he would return and take her to Topeka after picking up another passenger. Glad to be rid of the strange young woman, he drove away with no intention of returning.

Hoffman drove off to visit the friends he stayed with when he was in Kansas City, Fred and Grace Cheney on Mercier Street. It was 8:30 a.m. when he reached the Cheney home. Hoffman spoke to Grace Cheney and told her the story of the strange, sullen, possibly suicidal young woman he had ferried from St. Louis to Kansas City. Hoffman told Grace Cheney that the girl had mentioned that she was heading for Topeka for a funeral. Those details prompted Cheney to recall a story from the prior day's *Kansas City Star*. She suggested Hoffman's passenger might be the widow of slain FBI Public Enemy No. 1, Ben Dickson. The term "public enemy" originated in the Roman Empire and was appropriated in the early 1930s by the Chicago Crime Commission, which used the term to identify menacing criminals like Al Capone. In 1934, J. Edgar Hoover's FBI began using the term to describe outlaw bank robber John Dillinger and later applied the moniker to its most wanted fugitives, like Baby Face Nelson, Pretty Boy Floyd, and members of the Barker gang. In late 1938, Ben and Stella Mae Dickson had been designated Public Enemies Nos. 1 and 2 by Hoover's FBI.

According to the *Kansas City Star* story Cheney showed Hoffman, accused bank robber Dickson was shot by FBI special agents in St. Louis early on the evening of April 6. Cheney showed Hoffman the picture of Dickson's wife and "gun moll," Stella, that had appeared in the previous day's *Star*. The accompanying Associated Press story quoted FBI agents who claimed the young woman was armed and extremely dangerous, just as dangerous, in fact, as her "murderous" husband had been. The newspaper photograph bore some resemblance to Stella, but Hoffman was not certain it was his passenger. Under the front seat of the Buick, Hoffman had stashed a copy of the April 7 *St. Louis Post-Dispatch*, which he had been reading the previous day before departing for Kansas City. On the front page was another photo that was a better likeness of the young woman he had brought to Kansas City. Certain it was the same girl, Hoffman telephoned the Kansas City FBI office and spoke to Special Agent in Charge (SAC) Edward P. Guinane, who urged him to come to the Bureau office for an interview.

Rather than go directly to the Bureau office, Hoffman decided to see if he could find Stella, whom he had dropped off downtown near the FBI office just an hour before. Hoffman, accompanied by Grace Cheney, returned to the bus station but did not find her there. Demonstrating that he was a good amateur sleuth, Hoffman began checking nearby travel bureaus under the assumption that Stella was looking to hire another driver for the sixty-five-mile trip to Topeka. Hoffman found Stella at the A and A Travel Bureau at 1422 Main Street. Hoffman told Stella he would take her to Topeka but that he and his passenger first had to pick up a third passenger. With Cheney in the front seat and Stella in the back, Hoffman drove downtown and parked on Tenth Street between Grand Avenue and Walnut Street, about one and one-half blocks from the Kansas City FBI office, located at 811 Grand Avenue in the blocky, art deco US Courthouse and Post Office.

Hoffman left Cheney in the car with Stella and told them he would bring back the third passenger. Stella sat quietly in the backseat as Hoffman returned a few minutes later, leading SAC Guinane, along with Special Agents R. H. Hallenberg, F. G. McGeary, and H. O. Hawkins, back to the car. Because the car was parked on a busy street, the agents kept their revolvers holstered both to avoid drawing attention to themselves and out of concern for the safety of passersby. Upon reaching the car, Guinane went around to the passenger side while the other three agents stayed on the driver's side. Guinane leaned in the open window and asked the young woman her name. She claimed to be Gloria Cameron and said that she was from Topeka. Guinane took her purse and ordered her to step out of the car. Heartsick and exhausted, sixteen-year-old Stella Mae Dickson, whom the FBI had described just twenty-four hours before as a "dangerous gun moll," was taken into custody without incident. She was unarmed and wore a dirty dress and shabby overcoat. Once they reached the FBI office located in the federal building about one and one-half blocks from where Hoffman had parked, she admitted her true identity. Stella told FBI Agent L. B. Reed that after seeing her husband killed, she "just wanted to get home to mother."

2

BEN

On Monday, June 19, 1922, ten-year-old Ben Dickson and his twelve-year-old brother, Spencer, were playing in Topeka's Central Park.[1] The Dickson boys lived with their parents, James D. Dickson and Bertha J. Dickson, known as "Alma," along with brother Darwin in a tidy, modest home six blocks from Central Park. The narrow, 1.5-acre park is bounded by Southwest Clay Street on the west and Southwest Central Park Avenue on the east and lies between Thirteenth Avenue and Sixteenth Avenue. It is located less than a mile southwest of the imposing Kansas State Capitol building and almost directly south of the distinctive, gothic Topeka High School, completed in 1931, that features an ornate, 165-foot carillon tower. James Dickson was a respected chemistry teacher and administrator at Topeka High School from 1908 to 1943. Washburn College was also located in the same neighborhood as Central Park.

Central Park was built on land sold to the city by Dr. John Mc-Clintock for one dollar in 1899. Beginning in 1901, the city began developing the park, building three ponds that ran the full length of the narrow, one-block-wide park. The southernmost pond had an island in the center, and all three ponds were stocked with fish. The entire park was crisscrossed with walking paths and flower beds and trees. Swans and ducks nested around the ponds. Central Park provided a small but pleasant oasis in the center of the city. By the 1920s, Central Park was considered an important visitor destination and a safe place for neighborhood children to play. Ben and Spencer were both Boy Scouts, members of Troop 22. Ben eventually spent eight years in the Boy Scouts and "did a good deed every day," according to older brother Darwin.[2] A family scrapbook included a picture of Ben in his scouting uniform smiling as he admired a prize-winning pie he had baked. When he died in 1939, the Boy Scout fleur-de-lis crest was carved into Ben's grave marker.

On June 19, 1922, the two boys applied what they had learned in scouting ("Be Prepared, Do a Good Turn Daily") when they saw an elderly woman, apparently trying to commit suicide, drowning in one of the Central Park ponds. The woman had stopped to speak to the boys, who were sailing toy boats in the pond. She asked them whether the water was deep enough to drown a person. When they answered that they supposed it was, she walked a few feet away down the shore and threw herself in the water. Ben shouted to a man walking by and Spencer jumped in, but the woman struggled to keep her head underwater and he could not drag her out by himself. Ben jumped in to help and together he and Spencer held the woman's head above water. Eventually the man walking by reluctantly waded in to grab the three of them and pull them to the shore. The June 20, 1922, *Topeka State Journal* featured a drawing of the boys on its front page with a story headlined "Spencer and Ben Dickson, Aged 12 and 10 Years, Start Early on Career of Life Saving." The stories did say the woman was known to the boys but failed to mention that the drowning woman was actually Ben and Spencer's troubled aunt. The story did include the details that Ben was just 4 feet 4 inches tall and the water just a few feet from the rescue was much deeper than that, indicating the real danger involved. The June 21, 1922, *Topeka Daily Capital* also mentioned the incident in a short story on an inside page. According to family members, Ben and Spencer were later honored with a commendation from the mayor of Topeka for their bravery.

Benjamin Johnson Dickson, said to be distantly related to the nation's twenty-third president, Benjamin Harrison, was born December 30, 1911, in Topeka. Bureau documents and newspapers later repeatedly misstated his middle name as "James," after his father. His mother, Alma Johnson Dickson, her maiden name the source of Ben's middle name, was a rural Tyler, Minnesota, native. According to news accounts, Alma suffered from serious mental and physical ailments by the 1930s and was sheltered, as much as was possible, from news about her son Ben. Ben had two older brothers, James Darwin, known as Darwin, who died in 1999, and Spencer, who died unexpectedly of a stomach ailment in April 1938. Darwin was the oldest. The family lived a conventional, middle-class existence in a two-story home at 517 West Fourteenth Street in what was then a nice Topeka neighborhood one-half block west of Topeka Boulevard and about five blocks south of the state capitol building. The home still stands, although the second story was removed at some point and many other houses nearby were demolished. In addition to the Topeka home, James Dickson inherited the farm where he grew up, 320 rolling acres of farmland near Auburn, Kansas, sixteen miles southwest of Topeka. The Dickson family, through Alma's relatives, also shared a small cabin near Lake Benton in Minnesota and a farm a few miles east of there, north of Tyler.

According to older brother Darwin, Ben and Spencer, born two years apart on the same day, December 30, were inseparable. They played together every day, Darwin said, and the boys often hiked sixteen miles to the Auburn farm to camp and fish. Like many boys their age, Ben, Spencer, and Darwin enjoyed going to movies. "Jimmy Cagney was the little guy, Ben's favorite," Darwin wrote in an unpublished family history in 1996. "I don't know if Cagney had any influence on my brother as a tough guy."

By all accounts, James and Alma gave their children a warm and supportive home where reading and education were valued and

Ben and his older brother Spencer were born on the same day two years apart. The boys were inseparable. This photo was taken in approximately 1920. (Photo courtesy of Richard L. Dickson, from the Dickson family collection.)

encouraged. "We had the greatest parents in the world," Darwin said in a 1995 interview with the author. "They were well educated and gave us a great life." Living Dickson relatives who never knew Ben but spent time with their grandfather James, whom they knew as GP, recalled him as a kind and generous grandparent. Ben was a handsome and athletic young man. Friends said he was a fair soccer and base-ball player and a talented boxer who finished first or second in several Kansas and regional American Athletic Union competitions. Another friend later told FBI agents that Ben was very quiet, seldom drank, never danced, and smoked only a little. Ben was the "little guy" among his siblings. Spencer and Darwin were significantly taller, and in pho-tographs Ben is often seen smiling broadly with his brothers. Later photographs show a handsome man just over 5 feet 7 inches tall and weighing about 140 pounds with piercing, light blue eyes, short, dark

Ben was a member of Topeka Boy Scout Troop 22 for eight years. This photograph was taken in approximately 1925. (Photo courtesy of Richard L. Dickson, from the Dickson family collection.)

hair, relatively narrow shoulders, slightly wide hips, strong arms, and powerful legs. Ben was later described by a prison acquaintance as very intelligent but stubborn and "cool and calculating in his reasoning."

Hoover and his publicists would later make much of Ben's stable family background after his criminal record became known. That the child of a respected educator like James Dickson could nevertheless become a criminal fit Hoover's oft-stated belief that crime and immorality were everywhere in society and that "10,000 Public Enemies" lurked even in comfortable, middle-class American neighborhoods. "The common belief is that most criminals are the product of poverty and slum conditions, but the story of Bennie Dickson's life contradicts such a belief in a rather positive manner," Hoover said in a news release titled "Interesting Case 7-2561," produced by the Bureau's public relations–oriented Crime Records Section and sent to hundreds of newspapers and radio stations in 1939. In typically strident, vituperative language, Hoover and his publicists asserted that Ben Dickson was one of the "most vicious" criminals ever sought by the FBI, an assertion that does not hold up under even the most cursory scrutiny. It was typical of FBI publicity that accused criminals whose exploits were publicized by the Bureau were demonized in the most strident terms. Some of them, like Bonnie and Clyde and John Dillinger, deserved the infamy they had earned through repeated acts of brutality and violence, including in Bonnie and Clyde's case multiple, cold-blooded murders. But Ben was a relatively small-time criminal who showed no indications of "vicious" behavior. Other than the fact that they were all branded as Public Enemy No. 1, Dickson shares almost nothing in common with violent and murderous outlaws like Dillinger, Kelly, Nelson, or the Barker gang.

That is not to say that Ben Dickson did not commit the bank robberies that later made him an FBI public enemy. It does appear, however, that an unjust imprisonment at age seventeen set him off on a criminal path that he could not, or would not, escape. Ben's troubles with the law began in 1926 when, at age fifteen, he was arrested for joyriding in a neighbor's car. Darwin Dickson described the incident

James D. Dickson was a professor of chemistry at Topeka High School from 1908 until 1943. This photo of James Dickson outside the family home at 517 W. Fourteenth Street in Topeka was taken by Ben Dickson in 1931. (Photo courtesy of Richard L. Dickson, from the Dickson family collection.)

Ben's mother, Bertha (Alma) Johnson Dickson, in 1923. Mrs. Dickson
suffered from a debilitating mental illness and suffered a breakdown when
she was finally told of Ben's criminal record after his death in 1939. (Photo
courtesy of Richard L. Dickson, from the Dickson family collection.)

in a family history he wrote in 1996. "One day some teenagers found [a neighbor] Mr. Hixon had left his keys in his Packard Straight 8," Darwin wrote. "Perhaps on a dare the fellows persuaded Ben to drive around the block. Ben forgot 'lead me not into temptation' and did just that. Hixon missed his car, police [were] called, Ben [was] booked and a mug shot was put on file." Darwin later said he wished Hixon had not left the key in the car, since that joyride around the block was the start of Ben's many troubles. For that minor offense, Ben received a sentence of one to five years in the Kansas State Industrial Reformatory at Hutchinson, but because of his age, the sentence was reduced to probation, the continuation of which depended on good behavior and regular school attendance. Once he was known to police, though, Ben was unable to stay out of trouble. In 1928, Ben and two other Topeka boys were arrested and accused of burglary and larceny under circumstances that are unclear from extant court records. One of the boys pled guilty to the charge and was sentenced to five years in the reformatory. The charges against Ben were dismissed on October 18, 1928, but prosecutors had already taken steps to revoke Ben's probation, claiming, in a novel legal argument, that he had violated the terms both "in spirit" and "technically." In a motion filed in January 1929, district attorney Paul Hein claimed that Ben was "in the habit of carrying a gun and staying out at all late hours" and that one evening, Ben borrowed his brother Darwin's car and "caroused around until half past three in the morning" before being arrested for disorderly conduct. Ben was in and out of jail during the latter months of 1928 and beginning of 1929 as the status of his probation was reconsidered in Shawnee County courtrooms.

Ben's next alleged crime occurred in July 1929, while still on probation, when he was accused of hailing a cab in front of the Kansan Hotel on Ninth Street, near the capitol in downtown Topeka, and then assaulting and robbing the driver. According to the driver, when the cab stopped at the assailant's destination, the driver, for some unstated reason, got out of the car and turned his back on his fare. The driver claimed he was knocked unconscious and robbed of eight dollars. The cab was briefly stolen and was then abandoned in front of the Kansas State Capitol building, just two blocks away.

During 1928 and 1929, Ben boxed as a featherweight in amateur boxing exhibitions in Topeka. One local boxing coach later told the FBI that Ben "had the heart and soul of a great fighter" and that he fought with guts and determination. Darwin Dickson wrote that it was Ben's goal to become a champion professional boxer. According to Darwin, it was Ben's reputation as a talented boxer, combined with the mug shot on file with Topeka Police, that landed him in the reformatory. Darwin wrote in 1996 that the cab driver and the assailant were both members of Ben's boxing club. Perhaps because they were beaten in the ring by Ben, they decided to get even, according to Darwin. The two men, in cahoots, framed Ben for a faked robbery that he didn't commit, Darwin said. "No wonder the driver [who knew Ben from boxing] recognized Ben's picture in the mug shots," he wrote. When Ben was found by police after the cab robbery, he had a set of brass knuckles in his pocket and indeed the driver "identified" him as the assailant. Ben's boxing background became an element of the case against him. Darwin also claimed that his brother was with him at the time of the robbery, an alibi that was apparently discounted by authorities. "He and I were eating and drinking a beer two miles from where it happened," Darwin Dickson said at the time and repeated that assertion in a 1995 interview. "[The actual perpetrator] called my mother to apologize," Darwin said in 1995, his voice breaking with emotion. "They sent [Ben] to a reformatory for something he did not do."

An FBI report filed nine years later suggests there was significant ambiguity about the identity of the attacker and circumstances of the cab robbery. After a description of the event, the author of the FBI report stated, "The details of the above incident had to be obtained from the former County Attorney of Shawnee County . . . in as much as the records of the Topeka, Kansas, Police Department do not reflect same [details]." While Topeka Police records of the incident were lost decades ago, the circumstances of Ben's trial also raise questions about his guilt. Ben refused to accept a plea bargain, and his trial in Shawnee

County District Court began on June 26, 1929. Unusually for such an apparently open-and-shut assault case in which the victim had identified the perpetrator, the presentation of evidence by the prosecutors and defense took two and one-half days. The defense case went on for two days and included the testimony of at least a half dozen witnesses. While no trial transcript exists, the defense no doubt offered testimony that provided Ben with an alibi for the time of the attack. Interestingly, the jury in the case deliberated for nearly three full days before returning a guilty verdict on July 1, 1929, on the single count of robbery in the first degree.[3] The length of the trial, the number of defense witnesses versus just one prosecution witness, and the difficulty the jury had in reaching a verdict suggest that the circumstances of the cab robbery were not entirely clear.

Tried and convicted for felony assault, Ben was given the choice of joining the US Navy or serving time in the reformatory. "I often wondered how his life would have differed had he decided to go to the Navy," Darwin wrote in 1996. When he chose to serve his time, Ben received a harsh sentence of ten to twenty-one years in the Kansas State Industrial Reformatory in Hutchinson. Reformatories, in which youthful criminals, aged sixteen to thirty, were given vocational training, were a mid-1800s innovation in imprisonment. The Kansas State Industrial Reformatory, located in Hutchinson in south-central Kansas northwest of Wichita, opened in 1895.

The Kansas reformatory was modeled after the nation's first industrial reformatory at Elmira, New York. In 1906, the Hutchinson reformatory moved to a dour and formidable new building with two cell houses connected by a rotunda that housed administrative and security offices. Additional cell houses were added before 1929. The authors of the 1929 *Handbook of American Prisons and Reformatories* noted that the cell houses boasted only rudimentary plumbing. Published by the National Society of Penal Information, which included on its advisory committee famed Kansas journalist William Allen White, the *Handbook* was considered a thorough and authoritative review of the state of incarceration in America. According to the *Handbook*, the eight hundred or so inmates at the Kansas State Industrial Reformatory attended high school classes taught by "guard-teachers" for two hours every night after a regular eight-hour workday in which they were taught trades ranging from farmwork to automobile repair, printing, tailoring, and machine work. The *Handbook* authors judged the reformatory as "serving its purpose as effectively as any in the country." While the reformatory did offer training and high school coursework, it was still a prison with cellblocks, barred doors, stone walls, and convicted criminals. Ben arrived at the reformatory on August 3, 1929, and was paroled into the custody of his parents less than two years later on May 7, 1931. Dickson family members asserted for decades that Ben was an impressionable seventeen-year-old who was embittered by wrongful imprisonment and easily influenced by the criminals he met in the reformatory and by the shady characters he met in amateur boxing circles in prison and on the outside, an interesting parallel to the kind of disastrously defining influence he later had on his teenage wife. "He sat in his jail cell and cried like a baby," Darwin Dickson said. "Ben was not guilty of anything to speak of in the beginning. After they put you in those places where they put criminals, it changes your soul. Everything you have learned becomes dimmed."

After his early release in May 1931, it did not take long for Dickson to find his way back to prison. On June 17, 1931, accompanied by two men, one of whom he probably met in the reformatory, Ben stole a car in Fort Scott, Kansas, and drove east with twenty-one-year-old George Lewis and thirty-five-year-old Chauncey Hotchkiss across the border to nearby Stotesbury, Missouri, where they robbed the State Bank of Stotesbury. According to Topeka newspaper reports and FBI files, only one of the three, Dickson, entered the bank with a revolver and carried out the robbery. While unconfirmed, it is likely that Ben met Lewis, a Tulsa native about the same age, in the Hutchinson reformatory. Their connection to the older Hotchkiss is unclear. Along with his accomplices, Dickson, who according to newspaper accounts did not wear a disguise during the robbery, stole $1,147 from the bank. The Dust Bowl drought conditions that plagued the Great Plains during the Great Depression helped authorities track the robbers, according to FBI records. The dust raised as their car raced along back roads led authorities to a farm northeast of Fort Scott owned by G. H. Staunton. Ben had been staying there with the two other men. Lewis and Hotchkiss claimed they were not involved in the robbery, but $1,044 taken in the robbery was found on the farm. Lewis and Hotchkiss were arrested and gave up Ben, telling authorities they would likely find him at Gage Park in Topeka, where he liked to cool off with friends.

Gage Park, located in what was then the western edge of Topeka between Southwest Sixth Avenue and Southwest Tenth Street, opened in 1899 on eighty acres of land donated by the heirs of brickmaker and real estate investor Guilford Gage. The Gage Park swimming pool was a converted lake and, when the conversion to a swimming pool was completed in 1927, it was thought to be the world's largest "filtered" concrete pool. The pool was 460 feet long, 170 feet wide at its widest, and included an electric fountain, multiple slides and chutes, and even a sandy beach. The massive pool closed in 1956, was filled in in 1963, and the site was converted into a parking lot. The pool's ornate bathhouse was converted into a community theater in 1965.

On Saturday, June 20, 1931, Shawnee County Sheriff Wayne Horning and three deputies approached Ben in the Gage Park bathhouse. Bureau accounts, gathered thirdhand and years after the events, claimed that Ben had somehow stashed a revolver in his bathing suit. "Dickson reached under his bathing suit and secured a revolver which he leveled at an officer," the FBI's 1939 press release stated. Reports in the June 21, 1931, editions of both the *Topeka Daily Capital* and the *Topeka State Journal* included the even more incredible claim that when approached by authorities, Ben pulled a Smith & Wesson .32 caliber revolver from his belt and aimed it not at police but at children who stood nearby gawking at the scene inside the bathhouse. He then allegedly punched the sheriff twice. Ben was not charged with any weapons violations or with assaulting a police officer. It does not seem plausible that Ben carried a gun into the pool, but perhaps he had one with him in the bathhouse. The idea that Ben would aim a weapon at innocent children seems highly unlikely, a detail perhaps made up by police to make Ben seem more menacing. While the full circumstances are unclear, it seems likely that local police and, later, the Bureau may have exaggerated the circumstances of Ben's 1931 arrest to help buttress the case that he was a "vicious" and even "murderous" criminal. Whatever the circumstances of his arrest, Ben was taken into custody and extradited to Missouri the following day. He was identified by the bank teller, pled guilty to bank robbery charges, and on June 30, 1931, less than two months after he emerged from the Kansas State Industrial Reformatory, Ben began serving a ten-year sentence in the dismal Missouri State Penitentiary, in Jefferson City.

The Missouri State Penitentiary, known as "The Walls," opened in 1836. The penitentiary was nicknamed "the bloodiest 47 acres in America" by *Time* magazine in 1967 because of the alarming frequency of riots, murders, and assaults inside the walls. Located just a few blocks from the elegant Missouri State Capitol building, Jefferson City residents referred to the prison as "the big, the bad, the ugly," for its grim limestone exterior. Behind those imposing walls were five cell houses and several "dormitories." The interior grounds were haphazardly arranged, according to the 1929 *Handbook of American Prisons and Reformatories*. "In this respect [the ad hoc construction of the houses] the prison resembles San Quentin, California." The prison's cellblocks included the dreary, antiquated *Q* Hall. Built in 1868 and known as *A* Hall after 1937, *Q* Hall contained 152 individual cells in four dark, steamy tiers with narrow slits for windows. According to the *Handbook* authors, none of the cell houses were well-ventilated and the mustiness of the air was compounded by the prison's overcrowded conditions and one-bath-per-week allowance. Nearly four thousand inmates were housed inside The Walls. In contrast to the reformatories for youthful offenders that became a focus of rehabilitative justice in the early 1900s, no classes and only minimal vocational training programs were offered to inmates, who instead spent their time working in prison industries under harsh conditions. According to the *Handbook* authors in 1929:

The Missouri Prison is chiefly notable for its defects. These are to be found in the organization of its government, the very serious overcrowding, in low sanitary standards throughout the institution, in bad working conditions in the shops, in the medical program of both the general and tuberculosis hospitals, in the methods of disciplines, and in the lack of educational program. It is difficult to find any features of the prison which can be commended in themselves or compared favorably with like features in other institutions.

The *Handbook* authors noted that most inmates in Jefferson City were serving relatively short terms and were not considered violent offenders. The report authors concluded that because of its poor facilities and harsh treatment of inmates, the Missouri State Penitentiary was little more than an advanced crime school with the potential to transform its inmates into more dangerous criminals once they were released. "It is impossible to avoid the conclusion that the state, by housing in an institution such as this, first offenders and those whose offenses do not warrant a sentence of more than two years, is committing a more serious crime against society than the short-time inmates committed, and that the institution is doing more to contribute to crime in the state than it is to prevent it." The prison's most famous inmates over the years included James Earl Ray, boxer Sonny Liston, and Pretty Boy Floyd. Ray, sentenced to twenty years in The Walls as a repeat offender in 1959, escaped from the prison the year before he shot Martin Luther King, Jr., by hiding in a truck hauling bread from the prison bakery. The old penitentiary closed in 2004 and now hosts historical tours and, not surprisingly given its notorious past and gothic architecture, ghost hunts.

Ben was processed into the Missouri State Penitentiary on June 30, 1931, and was logged into the prison ledger as inmate number 39211 with a "merit time" release date of April 28, 1937. Penitentiary officials made a note of Ben's known aliases, which included "Bob Stewart" and

Convicted of a Missouri bank robbery in 1931, Ben Dickson was sent to the grim Missouri State Penitentiary in Jefferson City. He was released in 1937, his sentence commuted by the acting governor of Missouri. (Photo courtesy of the Missouri State Archives.)

"Dale Trent." Under "trade" they entered "stone mason." The category "rule violations" was left blank and that, along with a notation added later that one hundred days of additional merit time was taken off of Ben's sentence, indicates that he was a model prisoner. While incarcerated in The Walls, Ben worked in the prison library and participated in sports, renewing his interest in boxing. Ben made many friends and was a popular inmate, according to the FBI. One of his Missouri State Penitentiary "friends" would later turn Ben in to the FBI in exchange for a cash reward. No records of Ben's prison stay remain, other than the simple logbook listing inmates by admission date. Given the nature of the prison and its many incorrigible inmates, it is easy to imagine that six years, particularly six formative young adult years, inside The Walls would be a frightening and life-altering experience.

On January 19, 1937, Ben was released into the custody of his father, his sentence commuted by Missouri Lt. Governor (listed in the logbook as "acting Governor") Frank Gaines Harris. Ben returned to live in the family home in Topeka. In June 1937 Ben went with his brother Spencer to a Topeka roller-skating rink. Spencer introduced him to several people that evening as Johnny O'Malley, a new alias Ben had begun to use based on his mother's maiden name, Johnson. Among those "Johnny" met that night was a slim and pretty young blonde, Stella Mae Redenbaugh. Stella said later, "Johnny was gentlemanly around me and was nice to me and I learned to like him and we kept company together quite a bit." After a few months, twenty-six-year-old "Johnny" and fifteen-year-old Stella became "secretly engaged," she later claimed.

Depending on one's perspective, what happened next was either the foolish act of a recidivist or another example of Ben's bad luck combined with the corruption of local authorities. On July 7, 1937, Ben, who had been hired by a local cab company, went to Topeka City Hall to obtain the chauffeur's license required for cab drivers. The twenty-two-year-old examiner on duty at the Automobile License Bureau, Edward "Irl" Heidt (whose nickname was incorrectly reported in some newspaper and police accounts as Ira), allegedly taunted Dickson about his criminal past. Darwin Dickson told the FBI in 1938 that Heidt was "considered an obnoxious individual in his dealings with people," a judgment shared by several other people the FBI later interviewed. Darwin said that Ben "popped" Heidt in the mouth and tried to leave the office when Heidt jumped on his back and tore his shirt, prompting Ben, a hard-nosed boxer no doubt accustomed to defending himself in prison, to fight back. Heidt claimed that Ben attacked him without provocation, knocking him down and repeatedly kicking him, another story that fit societal expectations of a boxer and ex-convict. Ben told Darwin, "I had to protect myself. He was a nut." Once again, the details of the incident vary. According to a Kansas City FBI report, Dickson broke Heidt's jaw. Later FBI reports claimed Ben broke several of Heidt's ribs. Another Bureau report referred to the incident as a "tussle" and as a "scuffle." The FBI would later refer to the incident as an "attack" and present it as further evidence of Ben's "vicious" nature.

While it is impossible to determine the true nature of the incident, some combination of Ben's temper and Heidt's unpleasant personality resulted in another felony charge for Ben. It seems likely that Ben took issue with something the "obnoxious" Heidt said and punched the man, was attacked when his back was turned, and retaliated. Heidt, the loser of the "scuffle," may have embellished his story to cover up his part in inciting the incident.

Later on, as an explanation of how he had been persecuted, Ben told Stella that Topeka officials were primarily interested in his fight with the motor vehicle clerk because of Heidt's political connections, a claim that seems quite plausible. It was not uncommon in the 1930s for municipal police departments to be corrupted by the influence of local and statewide elected politicians. Heidt may well have had political connections. He was the son of Earl E. Heidt, a businessman who had once worked as the mailroom supervisor for Capper Publications, publisher of the *Topeka Daily Capital.* The founder of Capper Publications, Arthur Capper, was a Republican US Senator from Kansas from 1919 to 1949. By the late 1930s, Earl Heidt owned a service station in Topeka. As a local businessman who was at least acquainted with Capper, Earl Heidt could possibly have gotten his complaint given special attention by Topeka Police. Perhaps because of the Heidt family political connections and certainly because of Ben's prior convictions and his boxing experience, Dickson was charged with a serious and seemingly excessive felony, assault with the intent to kill. Faced with a felony charge, Ben fled to Kansas City, where the FBI later discovered he had frequented the Lido Club, a gambling club located at the corner of Thirty-First Street and Troost Avenue. Bureau agents also discovered that Ben lived with a girlfriend, not Stella, in Kansas City for a few months. Ben then moved on to Chicago, where he had family connections.

In Chicago, Ben stayed with two aunts and a cousin from his mother's side of the family. According to the FBI, he attended night school and began an American Athletic Union boxing career under his alias, Johnny O'Malley. Those familiar with his boxing career in Chicago and later in California reported to FBI agents that Ben was a tough, talented boxer. Dickson (as O'Malley) was licensed by the state boxing commission in Illinois, but no information about his win-loss record remains. Apparently, Ben dated a woman in Chicago and the Bureau later found a picture of him with the unnamed woman together at the Riverview Amusement Park in Chicago in front of a novelty backdrop, "Making Whoopee at Riverview." FBI agents even investigated the possibility that he had fathered a child with one of his girlfriends, although no evidence of that was ever found. In Chicago, Ben attended classes at Englewood Evening High School and worked for a vending machine company but quit when his supervisor began asking questions about his criminal record. Ben had one brush with the law during his stay with relatives in Chicago, when he and his cousin Bob Johnson were arrested on January 26, 1938, after an automobile accident left both men slightly injured. Ben's car slid on the ice and rear-ended another car at the corner of East Sixty-Sixth Street and South Cottage Grove Avenue, south of the University of Chicago campus. Ben, who told police his name was John Dickson, was driving the car at the time of the accident, the first of several automobile accidents during his time as a fugitive, and police found a revolver in the car. Johnson, who was killed later that year in a motorcycle accident, saved his cousin by claiming the gun was his.

Soon after the arrest, Ben left Chicago and traveled to California, settling in Los Angeles and registering as a student at the University of California at Los Angeles, where he took English and physics extension courses under the name B. John Dickson. Between March and May 1938, Dickson committed several armed robberies to support himself. According to Los Angeles FBI reports, Dickson robbed the Southern California Telephone Company in Huntington Park twice, getting away with $1,700, the Peerless Laundry twice, obtaining $240 and a revolver, and the Southern California Gas Company, taking $150. Later, the FBI would recover the Peerless Laundry owner's .38 caliber Smith & Wesson revolver among Dickson's personal effects. The revolver was likely the one held by Stella during two bank robberies. As he supported himself through crime, Dickson, as Johnny O'Malley, continued his boxing career in San Diego, where he also worked briefly as an elevator boy in the US Grant Hotel.

Bored, alone, and far from home, Ben corresponded with friends in Topeka and wrote to Stella, she later said, "practically every day." A rambling, stream-of-consciousness typewritten note to Stella, wistful and melancholy, was found among the couple's personal effects left in a recovered car and was the only one preserved in full in FBI files. The single-spaced letter suggests an intelligent but lonely man struggling to maintain a cheerful disposition.

Dear Stella,

Life is sweet again today for me even if it is cloudy and I have to wait at home all day for the fellow from Fresno. I don't know why but some days seem so matter of fact and just another day of this and that, and then comes a day like today so full of hope and peace and quiet that it evens up all the others. I think maybe writing to you has a lot to do with it because when I write to you I think of you so much and talk to you even if it is in the letter, anyway, it makes me happy. This morning I went down and bought a lot of candy and put it on a platter and in front of me, a constant temptation, but I am in training now so I can't eat much of it. I used to do that and sometimes that spirit of revolt at all bounds or whatever it is that makes me want to disobey orders or whatever it is that holds them, well in that spirit sometimes would get the better of my other wishes and I would then proceed not only to eat candy but the whole platter of it. . . . One's friends either make or mar their happiness and wherever one's friends are is a happy place and where they aren't is not a happy one, generally speaking. I can't find anything to take their place not excitement or amusements or recreation of any kind, only one thing and that is to get so engrossed in study or something that you haven't time to think of them, or else make more friends that take their place and that isn't easily done because old friends are the best. The reason people in strange places are so friendly is because they realize they need friends and want to make them. Happiness is in sharing and helping and giving rather than in selfishness.

Ben ended several of his letters with a postscript paraphrasing a popular song by Louis Armstrong, "Me and My Pocket Full of Dreams." Ben also practiced typing by repeatedly copying the text of favorite poems like "Invictus," by William Ernest Henley, and "The King's Picture," by Helen Barron Bostwick. *Invictus* is a Latin word meaning "unconquerable," and Henley's poem was a particular favorite for Ben, for whom its theme of persevering through adversity no doubt resonated. Ben wrote short paragraphs of inspirational affirmations based on that theme, apparently his own compositions: "The aim of life is to grow higher. When environment is not satisfactory one must change the environment or change oneself to become acclimated to it." Dickson's own poems and essays, like his letters, typically included themes of perseverance, loyalty, friendship, education, self-denial, and hope. The original material and selections of poetry suggest that Ben was an intelligent and emotional person who carried strong feelings for friends and loved ones and who keenly felt he had been the victim of injustice. Another common theme in Ben's writings is a desire to make up for lost time and atone for his mistakes. The letters and items later recovered by the FBI also demonstrate the influence of his father, James Dickson, as a teacher who valued education and even mailed books and directed his son's studies while Ben was on the run. Darwin Dickson said his younger brother was an emotional and loyal man and felt a duty to his family to "make something" of himself. It seems likely that he felt trapped by his prior mistakes, persecuted by police, and hopeless about his ability to "grow higher" and make his parents proud. Those feelings later provided the justification he gave his young wife for their two bank robberies.

It is also clear from the letters that Ben was lonely. According to an FBI report summarizing Ben's letters, he referred to Stella as his "sweetheart" and urged her to join him in Los Angeles. The timing of this long-distance correspondence is important in that it paralleled Stella's Halloween 1937 rape and subsequent treatments for gonorrhea in December 1937 and January 1938. In her discussions with case workers contained in her Bureau of Prisons file, she claimed that she went to California to meet up with a friend from school, not to connect with "Johnny." She told a counselor that she did encounter Ben [Johnny] shortly after she arrived in California but claimed that he was seeing another woman. She also told her counselor that it was two weeks after she arrived, when Ben had broken up with his girlfriend after a quarrel, that he impetuously said, "Let's you and me get married." Stella said later that she had not found a job in Los Angeles and that anything seemed better to her than returning to her shame in Topeka. She agreed to his proposal, but they did not marry immediately. Instead they moved into an apartment at 901 West 36th Place in Los Angeles, near the campus of the University of Southern California, but were unable to wed because Stella's age, just fifteen, required that a parent give consent for the wedding.

The two different stories Stella told—one that she ran away only to get away from Topeka and her shame and another that she ran to connect with "Johnny"—do not match. She may have altered the story she told the FBI to make her union with Ben appear more purposeful, more romantic, and less impromptu and opportunistic than it was. Given the shame of the attack and the sexually transmitted disease, it seems unlikely that she would have confided her predicament to Ben in her letters to him. In her FBI statement, Stella said that she and Johnny became close very quickly, before Johnny left for California, and were "secretly engaged" at that time. Given the trauma she suffered before leaving Topeka, she may have created the fiction of the rendezvous of long-distance lovers to explain why she left home. That fiction would have allowed her to avoid revealing to FBI officials the Halloween 1937 rape and resulting sexually transmitted disease that actually drove her to run away and head west. No mention of the rape appears in FBI files. Importantly, she ran away not into Ben's arms in Los Angeles but first stayed with a friend, the friend who had been with her the night she

Ben and Stella in April 1938 at their rented home in Los Angeles. (Photo courtesy of Richard L. Dickson, from the Dickson family collection.)

was raped, in Stockton. That fact alone indicates that meeting up with Johnny may have been something less than a carefully planned, long-awaited romantic reconnection. It seems most likely that their reunion in California was as much or more a matter of chance than a planned romantic rendezvous.

Whatever the circumstances that brought them together, Ben and Stella lived in Los Angeles for two months in their apartment near the University of Southern California campus. On April 30, 1938, about the time they were settling into a home in Los Angeles, Ben's beloved brother Spencer died suddenly and unexpectedly from a stomach ailment, described in FBI files as a bowel blockage. According to Ben's nephew Richard Dickson, the family had religious objections to modern medical treatment, a factor that may have contributed to Spencer's sudden death before his thirtieth birthday.[4] Spencer had married Lillie Marie Crites just three weeks before he died, and their son, Spencer, was born on December 17, 1938. Ben was unable, probably because he was being actively sought by Topeka Police, to return home for his brother's funeral. A few weeks after Spencer's death, though, early in the summer of 1938, Ben and Stella returned to Topeka. Stella stayed with her mother for two weeks while Ben traveled to Detroit to visit his cousin Bob Johnson in the hospital. Bob had been severely injured in a motorcycle accident, had had a leg amputated, and would die on September 28 of a skull fracture suffered in yet another motorcycle accident. When Ben returned to Topeka, the entire Dickson family departed for summer vacation together. With Ben and Stella in one car and Spencer's pregnant widow, Lillie, driving the other car carrying James and Alma Dickson and Darwin Dickson's son Jim, the family drove to their primitive, three-room cottage at Lake Benton, Minnesota. The simple cottage lacked running water and electricity, but the Dickson family spent every summer there.

The town of Lake Benton is located near the South Dakota border in the extreme southwest corner of Minnesota along the shores of its namesake glacial lake. The town, perhaps three blocks by ten blocks in size, is located on the far southwestern shore of the seven-mile-long lake that runs generally from southwest to northeast. Platted in 1879, Lake Benton's population peaked in 1940 at 961 and has declined nearly every year since. During its heyday in the 1930s and 1940s, the town and lake were the home to several bustling resorts and a raucous ballroom dance hall. The Summer Resort and Pavilion opened in Lake Benton in 1917. It included a roller-skating rink, a fifty-foot toboggan slide that launched visitors into the lake, and a boat that transported revelers to the Showboat Ballroom for dancing or roller-skating. In the 1920s, South Dakota native and bandleader Lawrence Welk and his orchestra performed frequently at the Showboat. During the summers, thousands of people vacationed in Lake Benton. The Showboat, much diminished over the years, continued operation into at least the 1980s.[5] The Dickson family had a cabin near the lake. The cabin was a small, single-story shack located near the intersection of Highways 14 and 75 along the southwestern shore in a cluster of cabins separated from the lake by Highway 75.

Ben's older brother Darwin recalled the family trips to the lake fondly, remembering fishing, hunting, target shooting, carnivals, dancing, swimming, and boating in the then-thriving resort town. "We didn't have air conditioning and it got hot in Kansas," Darwin said. "There was a cool spot in the world called Minnesota. We'd load up the Ford, put a dog on each side and hit the trail. It was a real show-place with a big dance hall and cabins. We had a wonderful time." What was different about the trip in the summer of 1938, of course, was the presence of Ben's fifteen-year-old girlfriend, Stella. En route to Lake Benton, Ben had confessed his true name and identity to Stella, begging her to understand and to give him an opportunity to turn his life around. Even though she knew his real first name, Stella always continued to address him as "Johnny." Apparently, Johnny did not tell Stella about his criminal record until later that summer.

Lake Benton residents later told FBI agents they remembered Stella from that summer as a pretty and sophisticated "city" woman who was a better shot with a rifle than Ben. After Ben and Stella became fugitives, neighbors told newspaper reporters that the couple spent many

The Johnson and Dickson family cabin at Lake Benton, Minnesota, was
a small shack on the far west corner of the lake near where US Highways
14 and 75 intersect. The Dickson family spent most summers at the cabin.
(Photo courtesy of Richard L. Dickson, from the Dickson family collection.)

hours hunting or taking target practice. Locals claimed, after Stella's
arrest, that, using either a pistol or rifle, she could puncture tin cans
thrown in the air. Whether those stories of her sharpshooting ability were true or whether those anecdotes were created to fit the "vicious outlaw," "sure shot Stella," and "gun moll" memes that were later
flogged endlessly by the FBI and by reporters is impossible to determine. Several people from Lake Benton interviewed much later by the
FBI did claim to have seen Stella shoot and were impressed with her
ability. One man said he was target shooting with Ben and Stella and
Ben challenged him to hit a dove about forty yards away. He tried and
missed several times. Stella hit the dove on her first try. Stella later
claimed that the photographs of her brandishing weapons in Lake Benton that summer were taken for fun and were not any indication of her
shooting ability or familiarity with guns. The couple did go hunting

nearly every day during those weeks, she said. One photo in particular, showing Stella aiming a pistol while holding a rifle, was reprinted hundreds of times in newspapers nationwide and probably did more to establish her "gun moll" credentials than anything else published about her in 1938 or 1939. Stella told FBI agents she was target shooting with the rifle when Ben handed her the pistol and told her to pose for the photo. The photo of Stella with the guns and many others, including photos of the attractive couple standing on the shore in their bathing suits, were later recovered from suitcases the Dicksons abandoned at a tourist camp in Topeka in November 1938. The FBI released many of the photos to newspapers and those two images in particular, Stella with guns and the couple in their bathing suits, became ubiquitous images of the "gangster" couple. Clearly, those photos were selected for release by Bureau publicists for their value in creating impressions of Stella as an attractive, morally questionable gun moll. Later that year, FBI agents found additional photographs from the summer trips to Lake Benton in a car abandoned by the couple near Vicksburg, Michigan.

When Ben and Stella weren't having fun outdoors at Lake Benton, James Dickson made sure his son was indoors studying. The continuation of his reading was a recurring theme in James's letters to Ben during his time as a fugitive. Bureau agents found books in every stash of personal items they recovered during their hunt for the Dicksons. At Lake Benton, Stella told FBI agents, Ben studied under his father's tutelage eight hours a day. For Stella, it must have been comforting to be accepted by a loving family and to be away from the harsh judgment of her friends and neighbors in Topeka. Similarly, the summer at Lake Benton was undoubtedly a respite for Ben from the judgment of police who still sought him for the Heidt assault. For Ben and Stella, the summer months in Lake Benton must have been among the best of their times together, although she later told a friend that the summer on the lake included a miscarriage of an early pregnancy, brought on by intensive physical activity. Stella's surviving relatives believe the miscarriage story was false and that Stella may have given birth to a child, probably in early 1939. The family's claims are bolstered by one summer 1938 picture of Stella doing laundry where she appears, according to family members, "larger than they ever saw her." In addition, Richard Araiza, the son of Stella's half sister Virginia, said his mother told him that Stella's child was put up for adoption and that she later hired a private investigator in a fruitless effort to find the child.[6] Given that Ben and Stella first lived together in Los Angeles in April 1938, it seems possible that a child might have been born in January or February in New Orleans. In that case, it is likely that Stella turned to her mother for advice, and perhaps based on that counsel the child was put up for adoption. The birth is all but impossible to confirm, but the family's story does seem plausible. If it is true, the loss of her child with Ben (no doubt she presumed they would have the opportunity to have more children later) adds one more layer of tragedy to Stella's sad story.

Toward the end of the summer of 1938, Ben confessed to Stella that his plan to get a new start in life depended on the cash they would get from robbing a bank. He admitted his prior convictions and convinced Stella that he had been treated unfairly by authorities when he was sent to Hutchinson. No doubt he used that questionable conviction to justify the Stotesbury robbery as an attempt to get his life back on the right track. Stella told FBI agents in 1939:

> Johnny told me that they could not be looking for him any harder than they were anyhow and he discussed with me robbing the bank at Elkton [South Dakota]. . . . Johnny talked about the fight he had with Ira [*sic*] Heidt and said he had been framed on that and if they got him back to Kansas they would send him back to the penitentiary anyhow and he was going to rob a bank.

As it turned out, Ben's confession of his criminal past and his robbery plans would have serious consequences for Stella's future. She later told one of her prison counselors that Ben had been a spoiled child. After his time in prison, according to the counselor's interpretation of Stella's comments, "he was then thoroughly imbued with resentment toward law enforcement and was filled with self-pity and felt that society in general was failing to give him a decent chance." The counselor added,

Ben and Stella Dickson, probably near Pipestone, Minnesota, in the fall of 1938. (Photo courtesy of Richard L. Dickson, from the Dickson family collection.)

"Those ideas he instilled in Stella and her mind now is so warped that she does not realize his fundamental weaknesses and that he exaggerated his difficulties to her." Having adopted Ben's victim mentality, Stella agreed to the plan to rob the bank, but first the two were married on August 3, 1938, by Municipal Judge T. E. Fellows in nearby Pipestone, Minnesota. Two strangers witnessed the vows, and the newlyweds celebrated their honeymoon at the Lake Benton cottage and at the Hotel Kimball in Lake Benton.

Darwin later said he believed that his brother was desperate for money and could not land a legitimate job because of his criminal record and because of the economic disaster of the Great Depression. Ben's brother Spencer also had trouble finding work, Darwin wrote in his family history, and traveled far and wide looking for jobs before landing an auto mechanic position in Chicago. Ben had entered prison in Hutchinson before the stock market crash of 1929, emerged for only a short time in 1931, and was not released from the Missouri

State Penitentiary until 1937. He had been in prison during the beginning and worst years of the Great Depression. By 1938, the economy was suffering from the second wave of the Great Depression, the so-called Roosevelt Recession that was sparked when President Roosevelt, responding to the political opposition, embarked on an austerity campaign, slashing government spending and thus pulling enormous amounts of money out of an economy that had been revived somewhat by the massive increase in federal spending in prior years. The economy had previously rebounded after the darkest days of the Depression in 1933, but the Roosevelt Recession erased most of those gains. The employment situation in the Midwest remained tenuous throughout the 1930s, the only decade in Kansas history when the state suffered a population loss, with most of those losses coming after 1935. Nationally, the unemployment rate in 1938 was 19 percent. Dickson had lost jobs in Topeka and Chicago because of his criminal record. He was also an emotional, impatient man living with the knowledge that he was a disappointment to his parents, who had created an expectation of success for their children. The fact that he never stopped studying or attempting to enroll in college suggests that in his mind he believed the financial boost from a bank robbery would allow him to make a fresh start. "That's when we lost him," Darwin Dickson said in 1995. "He didn't have any other choice at that time. He would get jobs and then lose them. The last time I saw him was in Kansas City in 1938. He was on the run and I didn't want to get myself tangled up."

3

J. EDGAR HOOVER'S FBI

The case of Ben and Stella Dickson came along in 1938, during an interim period between the era of high-profile midwestern outlaw cases and the onset of the FBI's focus during World War II on spies and the protection of the American war industries. Because the Dicksons outwardly fit the mold of the outlaws of the earlier 1930s, they were shoehorned by Bureau publicists into a category of criminals that included famed and murderous outlaws like Bonnie Parker and Clyde Barrow, better known as Bonnie and Clyde. The Dicksons' public image was constructed by FBI publicists more to showcase the Bureau's work than to reflect the reality of their crimes. The FBI promoted its pursuit of easy marks like the Dicksons in part to demonstrate the agency's continued utility and to drown out critics' charges that it became too powerful in the 1930s.

Those concerns about the power of a centralized law enforcement agency can be traced to the origin of the FBI. The Bureau of Investigation was founded in 1908 despite the fact that Congress, concerned about the potential for abuse of power and corruption, refused to authorize it. Instead, the attorney general issued his own executive order creating the investigative bureau within the Department of Justice.[1] Critics feared that a centralized federal police department would become populated with political appointees and carried the potential to be used, like local law enforcement agencies, as a tool of politicians. Just over ten years later, critics' concerns had largely come true. The first controversy to erode public confidence in the Bureau was its involvement in the so-called Palmer Raids in 1919 and 1920, in which ten thousand alleged radicals were arrested in mass raids based on sketchy warrants. Almost all were later released and the raids became a national scandal and example of federal law enforcement run amok. The Bureau's involvement in the Teapot Dome political scandal of 1921 and 1922 further confirmed critics' concerns when it was learned that Bureau agents had conducted politically motivated investigations of members of Congress. In 1924, the nation's new attorney general, Harlan Fiske Stone, an outspoken critic of the Palmer Raids, hired a new director for the Bureau of Investigation to clean up the agency. Oddly, the man Stone chose to clean up and professionalize the agency was part of the leadership of the corrupted Bureau, the assistant director in charge of the Bureau's General Intelligence Division, the man who had coordinated the discredited Palmer Raids, twenty-nine-year-old attorney J. Edgar Hoover. To his credit, Hoover fired political appointees, raised standards for the hiring of agents, initiated extensive training regimens for agents, and created an Identification Division in the Bureau for the storage and categorization of fingerprints, a science that had not yet caught on in the United States. Even after more than five years as director, though, Hoover and his Bureau were relatively unknown.

In 1930, the Bureau of Investigation, as it was then called, boasted just 339 special agents among its 600 total employees and an annual appropriation of $2.3 million. Its famous crime laboratory had not yet been created. Agents were not authorized to carry guns or make arrests but could only investigate a handful of federal crimes. Most agents were accountants or lawyers, not trained law enforcement officers. The

Bureau's director, Hoover, was anything but a household name. That year Hoover's name appeared only five times in the nation's agenda-setting newspaper, the *New York Times*. All but one of those mentions were related not to any particular investigation but instead came in stories about the Bureau's annual Uniform Crime Report, a statistical compilation of crime in the United States. By 1940, however, the Federal Bureau of Investigation and Hoover were American icons. Hoover's Bureau included 900 agents, 1,500 support staff, and a nearly quadrupled budget of $8.8 million. Agents carried guns, made arrests, and were responsible for investigations of dozens of crimes ranging from kidnapping to automobile theft and bank robbery. By 1940, the exploits of the FBI had been the subject of thousands of newspaper reports, magazine stories, radio programs, books, motion pictures, and even comic books. Americans knew FBI special agents by the moniker "G-Men." In their wake, Hoover's G-Men had left a trail of dead outlaws along with several heroic FBI agents who died in the line of duty.

The massive expansion of FBI jurisdiction was part of President Franklin Delano Roosevelt's New Deal that promised, among many other things, a War on Crime. The New Deal promised action on a variety of fronts, rather than the laissez-faire, limited government of the outgoing Herbert Hoover administration. Where President Hoover was viewed (fairly or not) as insensitive to the plight of Americans suffering from the economic disaster of the Great Depression, Roosevelt seized the initiative, pushing an alphabet soup of new federal programs through Congress. Roosevelt's administration began with one hundred days of transformative legislative action creating a whole series of experimental programs designed to pump money into the flagging economy. By 1934, FDR had turned his attention to crime, arguing that the "strong arm of Government" was needed to crush what the public perceived as a crime wave.

Initially, Attorney General Homer S. Cummings was the point man in the War on Crime, offering a Twelve Point Crime Program that increased the federal role in law enforcement in response to new developments that had given criminals a series of advantages. Fast

V8-engine-powered cars, including some that could approach one hundred miles per hour, allowed criminals to outrun police and cross state or other jurisdictional lines that stripped the legal authority from local police when they crossed them. Powerful automatic weapons like the classic Thompson submachine gun, known as the "Tommy" gun, that could fire hundreds of rounds of powerful .45 caliber ammunition per minute, allowed criminals to outgun police, who were typically armed only with .38 caliber revolvers. A new generation of interstate outlaws had learned to take advantage of those developments and was wreaking havoc, particularly in the Midwest. Cummings's program federalized many crimes, including kidnapping, racketeering, transportation of stolen property across state lines, bank robberies, and extortion. Under Cummings's plan, Bureau agents would be authorized to carry weapons, execute warrants, and make arrests. Many of those changes were wrapped into a Crime Control Act that was passed by Congress in 1934.[2]

Laws are merely words on paper, of course, and enforcing them is another matter entirely. For the newly named Federal Bureau of Investigation, charismatic and photogenic bank robber John Dillinger provided a trial by fire. Dillinger became a cultural icon in the early 1930s for his criminal adventures and tendency to embarrass the bungling law enforcement officials who attempted to find, capture, and imprison him. On May 7, 1934, *Time* magazine ran a four-page feature on Dillinger headlined "Bad Man at Large" that quoted Dillinger's father, who claimed, "John is a good boy." A high school dropout, Dillinger served nine years in an Indiana prison; almost immediately upon his release, he robbed an Ohio bank, kicking off an eight-month crime spree that captured headlines nationwide. Arrested for the Ohio robbery, his notoriety spiked after he escaped from a county jail in Lima, Ohio, on October 12, 1933. The local sheriff was murdered during that escape. Dillinger and his gang robbed police arsenals and then killed a police officer during an East Chicago, Indiana, bank robbery before they were captured in Tucson, Arizona, on January 23, 1934. Extradited to Crown Point, Indiana, Dillinger again escaped, brandishing a wooden

President Franklin Delano Roosevelt signs several crime bills that expanded the jurisdiction and powers of the FBI, then known as the Bureau of Investigation. Looking on from the left are Attorney General Homer S. Cummings, J. Edgar Hoover, Democratic senator Harry F. Ashurst of Arizona, and Assistant Attorney General Joseph B. Keenan. (Courtesy of the National Archives at College Park, Record Group 65H, Box 2, Folder 206, #1.)

gun he had carved himself and eluding an army of officers surrounding the jail. All of the above occurred before the FBI even got its permanent name. Hoover's agency, then briefly known as the Division of Investigation, was drawn into the Dillinger case only when the outlaw, after his Crown Point escape, stole a car and transported it across a state line, a violation of the Dyer Act of 1919 and one of the federal crimes investigated and enforced by Hoover's agents.

The first high-profile effort by Hoover's agency to capture Dillinger ended in disaster. On April 22, 1934, agents received a tip that Dillinger and his gang, which then included Lester Gillis, better known as Baby Face Nelson, had gathered at the Little Bohemia Lodge in northern Wisconsin. Hoping to capitalize on publicity about his agency's glorious capture of Dillinger, Hoover let the news slip to newsmen, who were told that "good news" was forthcoming in the Dillinger hunt. The results of the "raid" were anything but good news. Agents mistook innocent guests at the lodge for the Dillinger gang, killing one man and wounding two others in a hail of gunfire. Alerted by the gunfire, the Dillinger gang escaped out the back of the lodge, which, in a farcical tactical failure, had not been covered by agents. Shortly after the shootout at the lodge, Nelson flagged down two agents and a local police officer in a car a few miles away. When the car stopped, Nelson killed Agent W. Carter Baum, wounded the other two law enforcement officers, and took the vehicle. The results of the raid were disastrous, and thanks to extensive media coverage afterward they were an enormous embarrassment to Hoover and his Division of Investigation.

Hoover was not a public relations expert, but he well understood the disastrous message of the Little Bohemia fiasco. Hoping to jumpstart the Dillinger chase, Hoover dispatched Inspector Samuel Cowley to Chicago to supervise the search led by Special Agent in Charge Melvin Purvis. Meanwhile, Attorney General Cummings's statement that agents who located Dillinger should "shoot to kill—then count to 10" generated additional public interest in the case. On July 21, 1934, agents received a tip from an informant, Chicago brothel operator Anna Sage (real name Ana Cumpănaș), who promised to lead them to Dillinger. Sage was hoping to forestall her deportation and collect a monetary reward. Sage told Purvis that she and Dillinger would attend a motion picture at one of two Chicago theaters the following evening. On July 22, 1934, at about 10:30 p.m., Sage and Dillinger exited the Biograph Theater after watching *Manhattan Melodrama*, a forgettable crime picture starring Clark Gable and Myrna Loy. Purvis lit his cigar as a signal that he had positively identified Dillinger. The outlaw apparently sensed a trap and began running. Purvis warned him to surrender, but Dillinger reached for his gun, and in a less-than-textbook maneuver, three agents shot and killed Public Enemy No. 1 on the street and wounded two unlucky civilians. The shooting of Dillinger generated enormous media attention for the agency and for Purvis rather than Hoover. Sharing the credit for the Bureau's work was something Hoover disliked enough that he eventually pushed Purvis out of the FBI.

Next up on the list of high-profile public enemies was Charles "Pretty Boy" Floyd, shot by local police in Ohio on October 22, although Purvis and other agents on the scene took credit for the shooting. The killing of Baby Face Nelson a few months later, after Nelson killed Cowley and another agent, once again generated nationwide headlines. In early 1935, FBI agents traced members of a kidnapping gang led by Ma Barker to Florida, and she and son Fred were dispatched in a gunfight. The other leader of the Barker-Karpis gang, Alvin "Creepy" Karpis, was captured by FBI agents on May 1, 1936. Hoover himself was at the scene, and after Karpis was subdued, the director was brought in to "capture" him again as a public relations stunt. Those outlaw cases helped make the FBI a household name, something the Bureau was able to begin to capitalize on when Hoover created a public relations unit, the Crime Records Section, in 1935.

It was Louis B. Nichols, a former YMCA publicity man, who made the Crime Records Section among the most important units in the FBI. Nichols set public relations policies and, through his networking skills, created relationships with journalists and members of Congress that paid dividends for decades. Crime Records was among the most important sections in the FBI because of its successful efforts to respond to public questions and promote the Bureau's work through the news and entertainment media. During the 1930s alone, thousands of newspaper and magazine stories, radio programs, movies, and books about the FBI were produced by the Crime Records Section. Crime Records leveraged the compelling narratives of the FBI's outlaw cases to create essentially a public relations template for the Bureau. When Crime

Records assisted writers on stories, those stories tended to conform to a particular structure, featuring evidence of scientific law enforcement, an emphasis on the responsibility and utility of the Bureau, and a focus on Hoover as the great protector of American civil liberties.

Indeed, the FBI was a pioneer in the use of science in law enforcement, although it was far more common for informants than for lab work to help the Bureau solve crimes. The question of the Bureau's utility was indisputable, at least when it focused its attention solely on enforcing federal law rather than gathering political intelligence. As to the question of Hoover as a protector of civil liberties, the historical record is unequivocal in its judgment of the falsehood of that claim. Hoover's Bureau spied on dissenting Americans for decades. Nevertheless, those themes of science, utility, and Hoover-as-protector were promoted endlessly, and when they were wrapped around the inherently dramatic, life-and-death stories of outlaws like Dillinger and the rest, the public could not get enough. The mostly midwestern outlaws, with their outlandish antics, flamboyant style, brazen robberies, and sometimes violent endings, had become legendary figures in American culture, and Hoover's FBI took advantage of that opportunity. Between 1930 and 1940, the Bureau was transformed from an unknown agency into an iconic symbol of American law and order led by a director who himself became an icon and led the FBI until his death in 1972.[3]

The Dickson case was the last of the high-profile outlaw cases of the 1930s, occurring as it did just before the shift in Bureau interest from outlaws to World War II spies in 1940 and then to Communists in the postwar era. In 1938 and 1939, though, the Dickson case was the subject of hundreds of newspaper stories nationwide, prompted by the even more numerous press releases the Crime Records Section issued in connection with the investigation, code-named "Bendick," and eventually producing thousands of pages of documentation in FBI files. By the late 1930s, effective public relations, combined with notable arrests and shootings that captured the public's imagination, had made Hoover's FBI one of the most high-profile government agencies. Hoover was one of the most famous men in America, and his G-Men were viewed by the public as professional, trustworthy public servants in America's indispensable agency. Ben and Stella could not have chosen a worse moment to rob two South Dakota banks. In so doing, they positioned themselves as Dillinger and the other earlier 1930s outlaws had, as useful props in Hoover's public relations campaign.

4

TIME LOCK BANDITS

Three young girls played on Elk Street in Elkton, South Dakota, early on the afternoon of Thursday, August 25, 1938. It was the day before Stella Mae Dickson's sixteenth birthday. Elk Street was the community's main street, a wide thoroughfare that reflected the optimism of its founders, who believed it would one day be a much larger community. One of the girls playing on the street that day, Betty Walsh, then twelve, later told special agents of the FBI that at about two o'clock in the afternoon she had seen a young woman get out of a dirty, oil-streaked 1936 Ford with California license plates. The pretty young woman's "manner of walk and her actions" attracted the attention of Walsh, thirteen-year-old Jean Severson, and an unidentified third girl. Severson told the FBI that the young woman "had pronounced hip movement when she walked." The young woman, Stella Mae Dickson, was dressed in men's overalls and wore a straw hat and dark glasses. She carried a small package wrapped in newspaper and tied with string. The package was about the size of a machine gun, Walsh reported after the robbery, a comment playing into and perhaps reflecting the gun moll publicity in the aftermath that day. In fact, the newspaper concealed a long-barreled .38 caliber revolver. Walsh even claimed she jokingly told her friends the woman "may be a gun moll." Because of her shabby attire, Walsh said, the girls also thought perhaps the woman might be a hitchhiker or a hobo.[1]

Walsh's second supposition was well founded. Thousands of Americans with nothing to tie them down traveled throughout the country during the Great Depression. Some of those wanderers in search of opportunity even turned up on the streets of Elkton, a typical midwestern farming town in eastern South Dakota, less than a mile from the South Dakota–Minnesota border. Undoubtedly, Ben planned their shabby outfits to suggest that they were drifters passing through and thus would be particularly difficult for authorities to identify or locate. About one mile square, Elkton's north-south streets bore animal names: Beaver Street, Buffalo Street, Badger Street, Antelope Street, and the main drag, Elk Street. Like many small midwestern towns, Elkton was built in a sort of angled T-formation, with railroad tracks forming the upper crossbar of the *T* and Elk Street as the north-south upright. The community was platted in 1880, became home to a post office in 1882, and was officially incorporated in 1908. Named after a city in Maryland, Elkton's 1940 population of 779 reflected a nearly 10 percent drop during the Great Depression. The community's population topped out at nearly nine hundred in 1920 and has declined almost continually ever since. For Ben and Stella Mae Dickson, Elkton was a familiar stop, located just a ten-mile drive west on US Highway 14 and another two miles south on State Highway 13 from Lake Benton, Minnesota. Surrounded by cornfields, and about twenty miles southeast of the county seat, Brookings, Elkton's short main street was anchored by the Elkton Corn Exchange Bank on the northeast corner of Elk and Second Streets about one and one-half blocks south of the railroad tracks.

Ben and Stella had been watching the Corn Exchange Bank for several days before the robbery. After their marriage on August 3, they stayed at the cabin and then for a few days at the Kimball Hotel in Lake Benton. They spent their honeymoon exploring the area, settling on a plan for the bank robbery, and establishing a getaway route. The weekend before the robbery, the Art B. Thomas Carnival was in Elkton for a Gala Day. The Thomas Carnival company was founded in Lennox, South Dakota, in 1928, and by 1938 the carnival was bringing a self-contained festival to small towns across the Great Plains during the summer months. For a small, farming town like Elkton, located sixty-five miles from the "big city" of Sioux Falls to the south, a carnival was a major event, bringing people into town from the surrounding farms and communities for the midway rides, sideshows, and even a stage show. Several Elkton residents interviewed later by the FBI recalled seeing a "young, dark-complexioned" man and pretty young blonde woman at the carnival. At one point, according to witnesses, Stella even mounted the stage in the dance pavilion and sang a song over the loudspeakers with the orchestra. One witness said the song was something about "trees," while the other could not remember much about it other than his judgment that Stella "could not sing at all." That does not seem to have been the case. During its investigation, the FBI interviewed several people who had heard Stella sing, and all reported that she had a lovely singing voice. One Lake Benton woman who spent an afternoon at a beauty salon with her told the FBI that during their time together Stella "sang a number of songs in the Spanish language" and that she "had a marvelous singing voice." The image of Stella, then still just fifteen, mounting the stage at an Elkton carnival to sing provides a stark contrast to later FBI portrayals of her as a vicious gun moll or reporters' characterizations of her as "sure shot Stella." In reality, Stella was just a teenager, having fun at a carnival, indulging her love of singing and of popular music. One of Ben's friends in Chicago later told the FBI that Stella hoped to become a movie star. For Ben and Stella, the carnival no doubt provided a pleasant memory during the difficult months that followed.

Several other Elkton residents reported seeing the couple and the odd, oil- and dust-caked Ford on the morning of the robbery. In an attempt to make the car less noticeable, Ben had mixed some leftover paint and oil at the Johnson farm and painted the car. The still tacky oil-paint mixture became coated with dust from the dirt roads between Lake Benton and Elkton, making the car more instead of less conspicuous. The three young girls, Severson, Walsh, and the unnamed girl, were the only people who spoke to the Dicksons before the robbery that day. The youngest of the girls asked the shabbily dressed woman her name, but Stella just covered her face with her straw hat. "Further attempts to draw the woman into conversation were fruitless, and the trio, after noting the look of anger on her face, walked across the street to a store," the *Brookings Daily Register* reported a few days later. "Our plan was that Johnny [Ben] would go in the bank and rob it while I waited in the car," Stella later told the FBI.

At 2:30 p.m., cashier Robert Petschow stood behind the counter at the first teller window of the Corn Exchange Bank. The bank, located at the corner of Elk Street and East Second Street, occupied the south half of the building with an angled entry door at the corner. Like most small-town banks, the Corn Exchange Bank featured several teller windows and a work area behind them with a relatively empty lobby closer to the door to Elk Street. Petschow and the bank's bookkeeper, Elaine Lovley, were the only two employees on duty in the work area of the bank behind the teller windows. Petschow cashed a twenty-two-dollar check for Mrs. Walter Hurd. As Petschow handed Hurd her cash, he looked up and saw a man pointing a gun through teller window number two next to him. "This is a holdup," the man said. He told Hurd to stay where she was. At that moment, the bank door opened and fourteen-year-old Harold Belson entered the bank. Ben told Belson to stand next to Hurd and then asked Petschow how to get behind the counter and was directed to a swinging door near the front of the bank. Instead, Ben grabbed the frame of the teller window and swung himself over and behind the counter, John Dillinger–style. "How much money is in the bank?" Ben asked. Petschow said there was about $1,400 in cash. Dickson examined the cash book and then pulled out an empty, white, hundred-pound sugar sack and ordered Petschow to put the counter change in the sack. "Good old Nevada dollars," Ben remarked as Petschow scooped change into the sack. The mention of "Nevada dollars" later prompted the FBI to speculate that Dickson was a gambler, a supposition that their investigation proved true.

Ben then turned his attention to the vault at the rear of the building. The vault was protected by a time lock. Time locks, which saw widespread adoption by banks between 1870 and 1930, would allow a vault to be opened only on a certain schedule. The locks were designed to thwart bank robberies and kidnappings where a bank official might be snatched from his home at night and brought to the bank to dial in the combination and open up the vault. Petschow told Ben that the Corn Exchange Bank vault had a time lock that would not open until 3:00 p.m. "We will wait," Ben said and reached under the bib of his overalls to examine a pocket watch suspended on a piece of white string. He asked if there were any other employees of the bank. Petschow said there was one other employee who was away on an errand. Ben told Petschow not to raise his hands, go near the counter, or attempt to set off any alarms. The Corn Exchange Bank had only minimal alarm or self-defense systems. The bank had purchased two Manville electrically fired gas guns, designed to discharge a cloud of tear gas in the direction of a robber from a 37mm cartridge, but the buttons to fire those guns were not within Petschow's reach. Other than that, the bank's security was nonexistent. It contained no firearms and had no electric alarm system installed despite having been robbed previously in 1931.

Ben told Petschow and Lovley to act naturally and to continue working. According to them, Ben chewed on a matchstick and spoke slowly and pleasantly to them. His voice, they said, was not rough and he remained calm during the entire robbery. His plan was to herd any customers who entered during the thirty-minute wait into the workspace of the bank behind the teller windows, force them to lie on the ground, and hold them hostage until the time lock allowed the vault to be opened. Twelve customers came in while they waited. The second customer to enter the bank, after Belson, was a local farmhand, Theodore J. Schroeder. T. J. Herney, proprietor of the local pool hall, was next, followed by Lovley's sister Shirley. Next to enter was Stella.

Her entry, about fifteen minutes after the robbery began, angered Ben as she was to have stood watch outside. She became concerned when Dickson had not emerged after about ten minutes. "I got worried and went in the bank to look for him," Stella told the FBI. The fact that she went into the bank made later efforts to minimize her participation, and thus her sentence imposed by a judge, more difficult. Lovley told FBI investigators that she didn't even realize that the young woman was involved in the robbery until it was over. "Elaine Lovley advised that she did not realize that this woman was a bandit until after the customers and the bank employees had been placed in the vault and she noticed that this woman had not been placed in the vault," an FBI investigator reported.

Stella recalled:

When I went in, Johnny [Ben] was standing on the inside of the partition and was ordering people in the bank around and made them lie on the floor. He gave me orders and told me what to do so people in the bank would not think I was with him. Of course, the people in the bank must have known I was with him because they saw my gun [under the newspaper].

Responding to Ben's orders, Stella stood at the front of the bank, holding her newspaper-wrapped revolver. Nine more unsuspecting customers, along with bank president Lester Foreman, entered the building during the wait. As each new customer entered, Petschow recited the line as he had been prompted by Dickson. "This is a holdup. Just do what this man tells you and everything will be all right." Dickson met the customers in the lobby and sent the twelve men and one boy to lie on the floor behind the counter. The two women were allowed to sit at the counter.

During the thirty-minute wait, several "Robin Hood" incidents occurred. Dillinger had become famous in part because he was seen as a Robin Hood whose bank robberies were perceived as exacting popular vengeance on a heartless financial system that was squeezing Americans, particularly struggling farmers. In one instance, Dillinger destroyed mortgage records, theoretically saving farmers from foreclosure. Dillinger also occasionally returned cash to bank customers who, in his judgment, needed the money.

Roy Kramer, owner of the Elkton Standard filling station, was the sixth person to enter the Corn Exchange Bank. Kramer carried a deposit book and two checks. Ben noticed the checks as Kramer moved behind the counter and asked the man where he worked. Kramer told Ben he was a businessman and handed over the cash, checks, and his bank deposit book. Ben checked Kramer's bank balance and, apparently deciding Kramer needed the money, handed the cash and checks back to him. Mrs. Albert Koehn entered the bank at about 2:50 p.m. and was directed behind the counter. Mrs. Koehn looked like she might pass out from the stress of walking in on a robbery, and Petschow asked Ben if she could sit in his chair. Ben said yes. When Koehn sat down, she dropped the twenty-dollar bill she had intended to change. Ben saw the bill and asked Petschow who it belonged to. "To this lady here," Petschow said, pointing to Koehn. Ben handed her the twenty-dollar bill. John E. Dunn, the local postmaster and druggist, was the tenth customer to enter the bank. Dunn carried fifty dollars in cash and fifteen dollars in change. Ben took the cash and asked Dunn how much money was in his account. Dunn replied that his account balance was perhaps twenty-five or thirty dollars. After consulting the bank ledger, Ben asked the druggist why a businessman had so little money. "Is your business any good?" he asked. "It must be pretty bad." Again, he returned the money. "You can keep this," he said. "You probably need it as badly as I do." Maurice Campbell, manager of the Elkton City Liquor Store, received a similar interrogation from Ben. Campbell carried thirty dollars to deposit in a city account. Ben kept that money, reasoning that the cash belonged to the city, not to Campbell. Similarly, he kept the one hundred dollars in cash Robert Butler brought in from his father's grocery store, but only after Petschow checked the store's bank balance and found that it was more than $500.

At 3:00 p.m., Ben told Petschow to open the vault. When the time lock had not opened, Petschow told Ben it was not quite time. The two men returned to the front of the bank and Ben told his hostages there could be some trouble so they should keep quiet. "This applies to you, too," Ben told Stella, again attempting to maintain the ruse that she was not part of the robbery. After a minute or so, the time lock clicked, Petschow opened the vault, and Ben emptied the currency into the sugar sack. When the vault was cleaned out, he herded the hostages into the larger, rear compartment of the vault and down an inner staircase to a lower compartment. Foreman tried to enter before Elaine Lovley and Ben pushed him aside. "Don't you know ladies are always first?" When he shut the door, Ben secured the latch only partway, leaving a quarter inch of daylight between the door and its frame, probably imagining that the fully closed vault would be airtight. After Ben and Stella left the bank, it was less than ten minutes before another customer entered and freed the hostages stuck in the vault.

At 3:15 p.m., FBI Special Agent in Charge Werner Hanni of the Bureau's Aberdeen, South Dakota, office received a phone call from William S. Gordon of the South Dakota Attorney General's Office. The Elkton Corn Exchange Bank was insured by the Federal Deposit Insurance Corporation (FDIC), a New Deal program passed as part of the Banking Act of 1933. The Banking Act was intended to restore public confidence in a failing banking system. The FDIC insured depositor accounts against bank failures or robberies. Bank robbery of an FDIC-insured institution was a federal crime under the National Bank Robbery Act of 1934, part of a series of laws that dramatically expanded FBI jurisdiction. That phone call to Hanni began an eight-month investigation and pursuit involving hundreds of FBI agents across the country and generating thousands of pages of documentation in several Bureau files.

Ben and Stella escaped Elkton with $2,187.64 in cash, the equivalent to about $36,000 in 2015. When they left the bank, they drove a carefully planned, meandering route on country roads to the Johnson family farm north of Tyler, Minnesota, about seven miles east of Lake Benton. "We did not stop en route," Stella told FBI agents later. "When we got to the farm we parked the car out near the barn and

Stella Mae Dickson doing laundry on the primitive Johnson farm north of Tyler, Minnesota, probably in late summer 1938. (Photo courtesy of Richard L. Dickson, from the Dickson family collection.)

[Ben] walked up in the trees. He said he was going to hide the money." The Dicksons stayed at the farm for three or four days before returning to Topeka, where they stayed with Stella's mother and stepfather at the small Clay Street home. The house was so small that Ben slept on the back porch when they stayed there. During their visit they attended the 1938 Kansas Free Fair on September 16 and 17. Originally the Kansas State Fair, the Free Fair was created after a political battle in which the state fair was moved to Hutchinson in 1913. The Topeka Free Fair was held just blocks from the state capitol, and the late 1930s were among its most successful years, with booming attendance and expanding facilities and expositions. Hattie Redenbaugh said later that she and her husband attended car races at the fair with Ben and Stella and even sat next to three Topeka Police Department officers at the event. "Ben showed no fear of the law," Redenbaugh said. Ben and Stella memorialized their attendance at the fair with several novelty photos in "Tiajuana" scenes and included another woman, probably Stella's friend Elizabeth Musick, in some of the photos.

After the fair, the Dicksons traveled by train to Detroit, where they used some of their robbery proceeds to buy a new Buick. Ben wrecked this car in a high-speed crash soon after on state Highway 75 near Osage City, Kansas, south of Auburn. "Sometime in September 1938, while Johnny and I were riding with some of our friends around and near Osage [City], Kansas, we had a wreck in this car," Stella told FBI agents, adding that they were traveling ninety miles per hour at the time of the crash. Miraculously, no one was hurt. A tow truck took the car to a Topeka body shop where it remained until the FBI found it in 1939. The body shop owner told the FBI that the wreck was the worst he had ever seen. On October 1, Ben and Stella attended Bob Johnson's funeral in Lake Benton and then immediately drove back to Topeka. On October 11, Ben entered a Kansas City restaurant owned by Fred Stoufer. Ben told Stoufer's mother, who was working that afternoon, that he was interested in buying a car and asked if a 1937 Buick parked in front belonged to her. Ben seemed to prefer Ford and Buick V8-engined cars, probably because they were fast. Mrs. Stoufer replied that

Ben and Stella Mae Dickson pose in a novelty photograph taken at the
Topeka Free Fair in September 1938. (Photo courtesy of Richard L.
Dickson, from the Dickson family collection.)

"she would sell anything if she could make a profit on it." They agreed to meet that evening at about nine o'clock at the Stoufer home. Ben and Fred Stoufer took the car for a test drive and after a few blocks, Ben pulled over, drew his gun, forced Stoufer from the car, tossed him a one-hundred-dollar bill, and drove away. He did not return the vehicle and continued to Topeka, crossing a state line with a stolen vehicle. Seven weeks later, Dickson was charged in Kansas City with a violation of the Dyer Act for transporting a stolen automobile across state lines, another crime under the jurisdiction of Hoover's FBI.

Ben and Stella drove their 1937 Buick to Minnesota, again staying at the Lake Benton cabin. En route, Ben told Stella that their money had run out and that "it wouldn't be any worse if we robbed another [bank]." This time, Ben planned to rob a larger bank in a much larger community, Brookings, South Dakota. Located northwest of Elkton, Brookings was also laid out in a classic *T* shape by surveyors for the Chicago and North Western Railway in 1879. By 1938, Brookings's population of more than 5,300 made it one of South Dakota's largest communities. The city was named after Judge Wilmot Wood Brookings, elected in 1859 as the first provisional governor of Dakota Territory. W. W. Brookings was known for his two wooden legs, his own legs having been amputated due to frostbite he suffered traveling in a blizzard from Sioux Falls, South Dakota, to the territorial capital at Yankton. Judge Brookings never visited his namesake community. Brookings is the county seat and is also a college town, home to what was known in 1938 as South Dakota State College (now South Dakota State University), the state's largest institution of higher education. Founded in 1881, the university was originally known as Dakota Agricultural College, then as the South Dakota State College of Agriculture and Mechanic Arts. A land-grant institution, in 1938, South Dakota State College included five divisions: Agriculture, Engineering, General Science, Home Economics, and Pharmacy. The campus features the Coughlin Campanile, a bell tower built in 1909, standing 165 feet tall, and visible from miles away on the gently rolling prairie.[2]

The presence of the college and its students made Brookings a lively town in the fall, when football and particularly the college's homecoming celebration, called Hobo Day (so named after students adopted a lapsed University of Missouri tradition of dressing like bums for homecoming), provided a series of ready-made events for visitors. October is one of the busiest months in an agricultural and higher education town like Brookings and the city's busiest shopping area was the so-called Taylor's Corner, where Fourth Street and Main Avenue intersect. The pillared Northwest Security National Bank building, located at the southwest corner of Fourth and Main, anchored the intersection. From the large pillars framing its entrance to its narrow layout, tall windows along Fourth Street, and half-block depth, the two-story brick bank building, constructed in 1919, remains one of Main Avenue's grandest structures.

As they did before the Elkton robbery, Ben and Stella spent time in Brookings watching the bank. Ben occupied himself by learning the bank's routines and planning the robbery while Stella remained in their tourist camp cabin. They arrived in town on Tuesday, October 25, and checked in to a cabin at the City Tourist Camp located in Hillcrest Park at the southwest corner of Highway 14/Sixth Street and Seventeenth Avenue in Brookings. Tourist camps were primitive motels that became popular in the 1920s and 1930s as cars and roads improved and long-distance automobile travel became more feasible and comfortable. Typically, tourist camps featured individual cabins that looked and functioned like small houses. Many were heated in winter and featured electric fans in summer. The most "modern" camp cabins featured private bathrooms, kitchenettes, and even garages. While traditional hotels served primarily rail travelers, tourist camps were located along highways and catered primarily to the growing ranks of automobile travelers. The City Tourist Camp was operated by the Brookings Chamber of Commerce and featured several primitive cabins for sleeping only. There were few amenities. The camp included an outhouse, a single water pump, and possibly basic electrical service. The exteriors of the cabins were covered with thin strips of pine and bark from a sawmill nearby nailed onto the cabin frame to make

The Northwest Security National Bank in Brookings, South Dakota. Ben and Stella Mae Dickson robbed the bank on October 31, 1938. (Courtesy of the George and Evelyn Norby Collection, South Dakota State University Archives and Hilton M. Briggs Library Special Collections.)

them look like log cabins. The City Tourist Camp was torn down in the 1940s.[3]

The proprietor of the City Tourist Camp told investigators that the couple drove a newer, black two-door Buick sedan. They rented cabin number four and when the Dicksons refused to give a name, the proprietor wrote down their license plate number instead, Michigan U4939. The Dicksons stayed in the cabin until Friday, October 28, leaving at about five o'clock in the evening. The proprietor told FBI agents she thought their departure was odd since the town was gearing up for Hobo Day, to be held on Saturday, October 29. People were pouring into the town for the parade and the Jackrabbits' football game against the University of South Dakota Coyotes that weekend. When they checked in on Tuesday, Ben and Stella were the only guests in the cabins until Friday, when the camp's cabins and trailer parking grounds filled completely.

There were two other guests at the camp when Ben and Stella arrived. A man working on a federal project at the college and his wife had parked their automobile trailer at the camp. The trailer owners reported that the Dicksons left early, returned later in the morning, and otherwise left only to get meals. The trailer guests told FBI agents that Ben spent some time replacing the spark plugs in the car. The guests also said they saw Ben vomiting behind the cabin one evening. Stella appeared outside the cabin with Ben only when they left, except one day when she played with the guests' dog, exhibiting her love for dogs that later led the couple to buy a German shepherd in Roby, Indiana, for fifteen dollars during their run from police, only to realize they could not properly care for it. The dog, named Wolf, later was given to Hattie Redenbaugh. On another occasion in New Orleans, Ben and Stella picked up an injured dog and paid for the dog's veterinary care. During her later years in Kansas City, Stella's closest companions were her dogs.

The Buick was having problems with its water pump, and the Dicksons took it to the Dybdahl Garage, located on Fourth Street across the street and just west of the bank, to be repaired. Garage employees Ray Loe, Roy Bishman, and Virgil Braley told FBI investigators that the couple behaved strangely. Ben insisted on driving his car into the garage, a difficult maneuver most people preferred to have the mechanics do for them. The couple then refused to leave the car while the pump was repaired, possibly because they carried guns in the car. The Dicksons were also seen downtown that week by local jeweler Vernon Jackson. Later, when he saw a picture of Ben in the local newspaper a few weeks after the robbery, Jackson contacted the FBI and told agents that he knew the Dickson family from having spent time in Lake Benton. Jackson told agents that Dickson's father, James, was at the Lake Benton cottage as recently as the summer of 1938 and mentioned that Ben's mother's family had a farm in Tyler, Minnesota, just east of Lake Benton. Based on Jackson's tips, FBI agents were able to make a connection to Chicago, where Dickson's aunt Maude Johnson worked as a schoolteacher. Jackson's information allowed FBI agents to identify several of the Dicksons' regular travel destinations.

At 8:25 a.m. on Monday, October 31, 1938, thirty-five minutes before opening time, John Torsey, assistant manager of the Northwest Security National Bank, let himself out the bank's front door between the distinctive pillars, locking the door behind him. The bank was scheduled to open at 9:00 a.m. Torsey had a desk full of paperwork and told FBI agents he decided to walk down the block south to Tidball's Drug Store at 319 Main Avenue to buy a Coca-Cola. When Torsey returned, he noticed a dark-colored Buick with Minnesota or Michigan license plates parked in the third parking space south of the front door of the bank. Torsey saw a pretty, young blonde woman sitting in the front passenger seat and a short, athletically built man, his foot on the passenger-side running board, talking to the woman through the open window. While Ben and Stella had dressed like drifters for the Elkton robbery, they dressed formally in Brookings, perhaps in an attempt to confuse anyone who might link the two robberies. Dickson wore glasses, a gray herringbone suit, and a brown hat. Employees of the bank noticed a gold signet ring on the little finger of his left hand. Stella wore a salmon-colored coat over a blue-green dress and no hat. "The girl was pretty and neatly dressed," bank bookkeeper Dorothy Coffey told a *Sioux Falls Daily Argus Leader* reporter.[4] Ben and Stella had arrived early that morning, no doubt choosing the Monday morning after homecoming (the hometown Jackrabbits lost that year 7–0 to their USD rivals) for their robbery since they knew the town was likely to be quiet after the raucous weekend. They had coffee in the Tasty Shop at 320 Main Avenue, across the street and three doors south of the bank. The waitress there recalled that the two appeared nervous and kept looking out the window. She did not hear what they were talking about.

Torsey passed the parked car and walked up the three concrete steps to the bank door. As he unlocked the door, Torsey felt something poke him in the back. "This is a shotgun in your back and this is a holdup," Ben said, adding that Torsey should keep calm, open the door, and walk in as if nothing unusual had happened. Torsey said he immediately recognized the gunman as the man he had seen a few seconds before, talking to the young woman in the car. Once inside, Torsey, with Ben behind him, turned to the right and entered the bank offices separated from the public area by a pair of saloon-style swinging doors. "Keep right on going," Ben said.

Six tall windows on the north wall of the bank gave the space a bright and open feel under the high ceilings. The lobby was a long, narrow space along the south wall separated from the business area of the bank by a series of teller stations. Bank employees present that morning included the bank manager, Richard M. "Dick" DePuy, teller Curtis Lovre, and Coffey. Lovre left his chair at the check-posting machine behind the teller windows and approached Ben, who told him to sit down and "act natural." Ben walked up behind Coffey, took hold of her arm, and told her to sit down. Several times he warned the employees against sounding the alarm. He told them to remain calm and said that their lives were in their own hands. "This money's insured," he said, referring to the Federal Deposit Insurance Corporation that guaranteed depositors' money against robberies or bank failures. "So just behave yourselves." Torsey told investigators that Ben's shotgun had a sawed-off barrel and tape on the stock. There was a knock at the front door and Ben motioned for Torsey to let Stella in. Torsey did so and then moved back behind the partition while Stella remained in the lobby throughout the robbery, pacing nervously up and down in front of the teller windows in the long, narrow public area of the bank. According to witnesses, she kept her right hand inside the newspaper-wrapped package and rested the end of the package, likely the barrel of the long-barreled .38 caliber revolver she carried, on her left forearm as

Ben Dickson wearing the suit he wore during the Brookings Northwest Security Bank robbery. This photo was likely taken in Pipestone, Minnesota, shortly before or after the Brookings robbery. (Photo courtesy of Richard L. Dickson, from the Dickson family collection.)

she paced nervously back and forth. Dickson ordered Stella to keep an eye on the employees. While Stella later claimed she had entered the Brookings bank, as in Elkton, because she was worried about "Johnny," her early entry, before the bank opened, suggests that her role in the Brookings robbery was more significant, albeit again planned and orchestrated by Dickson.

While Stella watched the employees, Ben handed DePuy a white pillowcase and ordered him to the rear of the bank to open the vault. As in Elkton, the access to the vault was controlled by a time lock. A large round auxiliary safe stood outside of the vault. DePuy told Ben he did not know the combination to open the safe. Torsey was called back and reached for a string to pull on the overhead light outside the safe. Apparently concerned that the string might trigger an alarm, Ben flinched and told him to leave the string alone. Torsey pointed to the lights above. "Pull it if you want, but if it is anything but a light, I'll let you have it," Ben reportedly said. Once the area was lit, Torsey opened the large, freestanding safe outside the vault and began filling the pillowcase. Ben asked how much money was in the safe and Torsey responded, "Twenty," meaning the small safe contained $2,000. Torsey told the robber that the rest of the money was in the vault and wouldn't open until a time lock triggered. "When will it open?" Ben asked, adding that he assumed it would open at 9:00 a.m. "I'm not quite sure," Torsey said. "I believe it would be 10:30 a.m. or about that time." Ben told Torsey that nearly two hours was a long time to wait for the lock to open but said that he could do it. Torsey said the lock might not open until closer to 11:00 a.m. Ben replied that it had better open at 10:30 a.m.

Ben next asked about safe deposit boxes and was told there was no money or valuables in them. He forced Torsey to open several and, after finding nothing of value in those, the two men returned to the work area of the bank. While they waited for 9:00 a.m. to open the bank, Ben peppered Torsey with questions about the bank's operations. Where did each teller normally work? How much money was in the cash drawers? In response to an order, Torsey removed most of the money from each of the cash drawers, leaving ten five-dollar bills and some one-dollar bills in each to allow business to proceed. As the clock approached opening time, 9:00 a.m., two additional employees, insurance agent John Hanten and clerk Robert Flittie, arrived and were herded behind the teller windows and told to remain calm. Just before 9:00 a.m., Ben noticed a series of buttons and wires underneath the teller windows, part of a rudimentary alarm system. The buttons were connected to buzzers at a clothing store next door to the south and a pool hall in the basement beneath it. Ben asked for scissors and ordered Torsey to cut the wires. He did so, carefully, as Ben watched him closely. The bank had no other security systems and there were no defensive firearms or teargas guns in the bank.

During the Elkton robbery two months before, Ben and Stella made hostages of the dozen or so customers who entered, a strategy that worked in a relatively quiet, small-town bank. That same strategy would not work for the much busier Northwest Security National Bank, located in a regional agricultural hub and college town like Brookings. Instead, during the Brookings robbery, customers were allowed to come and go, transacting business as usual while Ben waited ninety minutes for the time lock on the vault to open. During that time, Ben stood behind the counter or sat in the office near DePuy, who remained at his desk. Stella paced the lobby. In the Elkton robbery, many of the customers and even some of the bank employees failed to recognize Stella as part of the robbery team. There was no mistaking her role in Brookings, where her odd and awkward movements were noticed by many of the customers. Ben warned tellers not to pass any notes to customers and threatened to begin shooting if he saw anything suspicious. He further instructed bank employees that if anyone asked about him, they were to explain that he was a bank inspector.

Between 9:00 a.m. and 10:30 a.m., more than fifty customers entered the bank, worked with bank employees to complete their business, and left. While some noticed that things were different in the bank, no one detected a robbery in progress. Decades later, Charles

"Tim" Monahan recalled entering the bank twice that morning, once to pay off a note and another time to change a large bill. He remembered a well-dressed, pretty young blonde woman in the lobby but otherwise noticed nothing unusual.[5] Grocer Cassius P. Wells said he went into the bank at about 10:30 a.m. and approached Lovre's teller's cage. Wells recalled that as he was conducting his business, Stella looked over his shoulder and he turned to look directly in her face. She turned and walked away. With Ben holding a gun at his side, DePuy "worked under terrific pressure during the holdup" and even processed and granted loans to six customers, each of whom sat at his desk, discussed their needs with the bank manager, and filled out forms to complete the transactions.

Raymond Rossman, a farmer from rural Aurora, South Dakota, a few miles east of Brookings, said he talked to DePuy for about two minutes and noticed the stranger closely observing the conversation. Another Aurora farmer, Alfred Chenowith, was among the first customers to arrive. Chenowith told FBI agents that he sat with DePuy for twenty minutes to process the renewal of some notes. Chenowith noticed a strange man sitting to the side of DePuy and that the man observed their conversation closely. Chenowith later described the stranger as a "hard-looking individual" but did not alert authorities at the time. A few minutes after Chenowith left, Leo Brenner, one of DePuy's regular coffee break companions, stopped in to invite DePuy to join their morning coffee klatch at a café down the street. DePuy told him he "couldn't get away just then." Thomas S. Johnson, a farmer from five miles north of Brookings, spoke to DePuy about a loan and noticed a stern, serious man sitting nearby. Johnson told the FBI "he thought to himself that as soon as he got out he would report the matter to the Chief of Police but was afraid he might be wrong and the laugh would be on him." When teller Dorothy Coffey saw her sister enter the bank, she quickly ducked behind the counter to hide. "She was afraid she couldn't fool her sister," *Brookings Daily Register* publisher Charles H. J. Mitchell wrote on November 7, 1938, praising Coffey's quick thinking.

According to the October 31 edition of the *Brookings Daily Register*, the robbery featured just one memorable Robin Hood incident similar to those reported in newspapers after the Elkton robbery. During a quiet moment when no customers were in the bank, Ben asked Hanten how much his topcoat had cost. Hanten replied that the coat cost twenty-five dollars. Ben took the coat and ordered Hanten to take twenty-five dollars from the cash drawers to cover the cost. Hanten did as he was told. He later tried to return the money, but DePuy told him to keep it.

At 10:30 a.m., Ben and Torsey checked the vault. The time lock had not opened. While they waited, Ben told Torsey to clear out the remaining change from the small safe. "You don't want the heavy stuff," Torsey said. "I want everything," Ben replied. As Torsey put the change in the pillowcase, the time lock clicked open. All of the money and securities in the vault, except for $500 in mutilated bills that Torsey missed, were crammed into the pillowcase, which was placed inside a second case after it threatened to split from the volume and weight of the cash. DePuy was called to the vault, and he and Torsey together carried the heavy double pillowcase to the front of the bank and put the remaining money from the cash drawers into the case. The Dicksons prepared to leave with the packed pillowcase holding more than seventy-five pounds of cash, change, and securities. Ben ordered Torsey to carry the load, but again, the heavy, awkward pillowcase was too much for him. DePuy was told to help and Ben laughed as the two men struggled with the seventy-five-pound load. Ben held the door open as the two bankers continued their tragicomic struggle with the heavy bag of loot. Other difficulties arose as they left the bank and walked three parking spaces, about thirty feet south of the bank door, to the Dicksons' Buick. "We went right over to the car and DePuy tried to put the money in the right (passenger) side of the car, but there was another car parked so close that he could not get through," Torsey told FBI investigators. "I hollered at DePuy and told him to bring it around the other side and he did so and the bandit followed him." Lewis Sinjen, a Brookings County farmer, was the culprit, having parked very close to the black Buick. He saw the Dicksons, Torsey, and DePuy exit the bank, watched them for a moment, and then, apparently deciding nothing was amiss, exited his car through the passenger-side door and entered the bank.

DePuy deposited the pillowcase in the driver's side rear cargo area of the two-door coupe. Ben ordered Torsey to stand on the right running board and ordered DePuy to stand on the left. As they began to back out, the car was blocked in by a passing motorist and the slow-motion getaway waited another thirty seconds while an elderly man moved his car out of the way south down the street. Finally underway, Ben drove south one block on Main Avenue, then turned east on Third Street. Two blocks east, in front of the Revell Apartments near the southwest corner of the Brookings County Courthouse grounds, Dickson stopped the car and told Torsey and DePuy they were free to go. As the car sped away, Torsey and DePuy looked up and saw Stella smiling broadly and waving goodbye out the back window of the Buick. Torsey and DePuy turned and ran west toward the bank. Torsey headed straight for the bank and DePuy stopped, red-faced and out of breath, at the Beatrice Creamery a block east of the bank to call the police.

Ben and Stella continued east, probably to Seventh Avenue, and then turned left and drove three blocks north to Sixth Street, the portion of US Highway 14 that runs through Brookings. Three blocks later, at Medary Avenue, the main north-south avenue in town at that time, they turned north, then east again on Seventh Street for a few blocks, and then finally back onto Sixth Street heading east toward Lake Benton. George Burgman of the White Eagle Filling Station, at the corner of Sixth Street and Medary Avenue, reported that at about eleven o'clock in the morning, a dark-colored Buick approached the intersection from the west traveling at about forty miles per hour, slowed down slightly, and turned north on Medary Avenue. As they made the turn, a young woman tossed something out the passenger window. Burgman ran out into the street and began picking up about twenty-five roofing nails scattered on the pavement, apparently intended to disable any pursuing cars. There were none. A few moments later, back on Sixth Street heading east and concerned that one of the nails might have punctured his own tire, Ben skidded the Buick to a stop at the Macomb Standard Filling Station located on the east edge of town near the City Tourist Camp. The proprietor, W. J. Macomb, asked if he could help, and Ben hollered that he thought he might have a flat tire, jumped out of the car, checked the rear tires, and finding no problem, sped away to the east toward Lake Benton and Tyler.

Even though they had dressed differently for the Brookings robberies, newspapers in Brookings and Sioux Falls reported the obvious similarities between the two events. Both robberies involved two people, a young woman and an older man. Both included Robin Hood incidents. And in each case, the bandits had waited for a time lock to open. The biggest difference between the two heists, other than the hostage taking in Elkton, was the amount of cash taken. While they had gotten away with about $2,000 in the Elkton robbery, the Brookings robbery netted the Dicksons $17,593 in cash, the equivalent of nearly $300,000 in 2015. In addition, their take from the Northwest Security National Bank included more than $16,000 in securities, including stock certificates from Standard Oil, J. C. Penney, Sears Roebuck, and Chrysler. Combined with the intrigue of an attractive man-and-woman robbery team, the huge haul from the Brookings robbery made the incident seem more mysterious and impactful and dramatically heightened public interest in the case.

According to Stella, they desperately needed the money. "Two days before we robbed the bank at Brookings, South Dakota, we slept in the Buick in the barn at the farm in Tyler, Minnesota, because we had run out of money and did not have funds with which to pay rent," Stella said. A few days later, FBI agents, acting on Vernon Jackson's tip, interviewed people in the Lake Benton and Tyler areas and found witnesses who had seen the Dicksons' Buick parked at the Johnson farm on October 30. One Tyler resident who had been hunting pheasants near the Johnson farm said he saw the car inside a barn and even approached the barn and peeked in. He saw a suitcase on the ground next to the car but did not see any people in the area. The money from the Brookings robbery was never recovered. Family members later speculated that Ben buried some of it on the Tyler farm, northeast of Topeka, or perhaps on the Auburn, Kansas, family farm. "Johnny told me that he took part of the money we got at Brookings, South Dakota, and hid it," Stella said later. "He never did tell me where he hid that money. I recall that he kept at least $2,000 of it because he always had about that much money on him." The FBI later recovered a notebook from one of the Dicksons' abandoned cars that included an accounting for the Brookings robbery money. According to the figures in his notebook, Ben gambled away $13,800 of the take from the Brookings robbery.

5

PUBLIC ENEMIES

At the Johnson farm, Ben again mixed some oil and paint to paint the Buick yellow (according to Stella, he loved yellow cars). From the Johnson farm, the Dicksons traveled southwest toward Topeka. Once again, Ben did not wait for the paint to dry, making the car more conspicuous. "Driving the car with wet paint caused a lot of dust to stick to it," Stella recalled. Aware that local police often watched their parents' homes, the Dicksons likely stayed at a Topeka tourist camp or at what the family referred to as "Ben's cabin," a boxcar located in a pasture west of Auburn, Kansas, southwest of Topeka. According to family members' recollections, the shabby, rustic cabin, located on the 320 acres of farmland where James Dickson grew up, featured a well for fresh water and an escape tunnel Ben had dug that led to a nearby road. Stella said that during the stay in Kansas, Ben buried some of the money they stole in Brookings, probably somewhere northeast of Topeka. After a brief stay in the Topeka area, the Dicksons again traveled to Detroit to shop for cars and obtain information to create believable aliases. Using a clever ruse, the Dicksons gathered detailed information from several people. It was a scheme they used several times, creating a series of about a dozen aliases that made the investigative work of the FBI more difficult. The scheme was simple. Ben placed a classified advertisement in a Detroit newspaper requesting applicants for a stenographer position. They placed a similar notice with a Detroit employment agency. Those who applied for the nonexistent job, particularly those of the right age who resembled Ben and Stella, became potential aliases. "We talked to a stenographer named Elva Clayton," Stella told the FBI. "Her married name was Smith. We did not hire her. We just wanted to get a name." While in Detroit, they purchased two used cars, a Pontiac and another Buick. Ben's obsession with obtaining multiple cars to maintain anonymity on the road ironically led to their first near capture, in Topeka in November 1938.

On their way to Topeka, Ben and Stella stopped in Crown Point, Indiana, site of Dillinger's 1934 escape from the "escape-proof" local jail. In Crown Point they were married, their second wedding, on November 22, this time under the names James Duncan and Elva Clayton. The marriage may have been part of an effort to establish a paper trail for their new aliases or it may have been a romantic gesture. Perhaps the marriage served both purposes. When they returned to Topeka the following day, Ben and Stella checked in at the Ace Motor Court, located north of "Dead Man's Corner," where North Topeka Boulevard and Lyman Road intersect in Topeka near Soldier Creek. By the late 1930s, Topeka boasted twenty-four hotels, including two for African Americans only, and ten tourist camps. Located near a busy crossroads, the Ace Motor Court was particularly well positioned for cross-country travelers or for a fugitive couple in need of easy access to high-speed roadways.

Topeka Police had continued to investigate the assault on Irl Heidt, an investigation that led them to a break in the case in late November. While investigating another, unrelated crime, the officers began asking questions about a Buick left at a Topeka body shop to be repainted. The car was registered to William Harrison. A body shop employee told police that William Harrison said he was the nephew of Topeka

High School teacher James Dickson, Ben's father, who had accompanied Harrison when he dropped off the car. On a hunch, police showed the body shop employee a mug shot and the employee identified Ben as the man who had dropped the car off for repair and repainting. The Buick in question was the car Ben stole from a Kansas City man and the same car used in the Brookings robbery, although Topeka Police had no inkling of Ben's involvement in that crime. Inexplicably, police did not put the car under surveillance, and when they returned a few days later, they found that the car had been picked up, the forty-two-dollar repainting charge paid in one-dollar bills. Continuing their investigation, Topeka Police found another of Ben's cars at another body shop in Topeka, dropped off under the name Johnny O'Malley several months before. That was the new Buick the Dicksons had wrecked months before near Osage City, Kansas. The body shop owner told police that a man fitting Dickson's description was staying at the Ace Motor Court.

At that point, Ben was wanted in Topeka only for the assault on Heidt and was suspected in the theft of the Buick from Kansas City. Given those relatively minor offenses, the police response and actions at the Ace Motor Court appear overzealous. Topeka Police, along with Kansas State Police and Shawnee County deputies, set up a stakeout at the Ace Motor Court on the morning of November 24, 1938. The Ace Motor Court was located at 2117 Topeka Avenue, just north of Dead Man's Corner in north-central Topeka. Topeka Avenue (now Topeka Boulevard) ran from north to south and led to a new bridge across the Kansas River that had opened earlier in 1938. A Walgreens and a Long John Silver's now occupy the approximate site. The motor court's main driveway ran east to west, with the far end of the drive dead-ending near the north-south portion of Soldier Creek. On the evening of November 23, 1938, Ben and Stella took Stella's mother, Hattie, for a ride in the repainted Buick. After dropping Mrs. Redenbaugh and the Buick off at the Redenbaugh home at about 11:30 p.m., the Dicksons took their Pontiac and picked up Stella's married friend Elizabeth Musick. Musick, whose maiden surname was Ure, was four years older than Stella and the two had been friends for only a year or two. The

Dicksons and Musick spent the evening in the restaurant at the Sunset Inn located across the street from the tourist camp. The proprietor told FBI agents that the three ate and talked until almost three o'clock in the morning and had to be asked to leave. Ben, Stella, and Musick then returned to the room at the Ace Motor Court. Musick stayed the night. Dickson had parked the Pontiac in the nearby garage, which was about forty feet east of their room. The three slept late and did not emerge until 2:00 p.m. on November 24. That afternoon, Topeka police officers and Shawnee County deputy sheriffs were stationed nearby, some in room number one and the rest in the motor court's office. A Kansas Highway Patrol car was parked to the south on Topeka Avenue.

Ben emerged from the cabin first, carrying a large, heavy suitcase in each hand, and walked east toward the garage. Musick and Stella followed a few feet behind. "Elizabeth and I were out of the cabin, and I saw some men start walking toward Johnny [Ben]," Stella told the FBI. Ben walked past the next room over and as officers poured out of there, Topeka Police Detective Bill Dowling emerged from the office and shouted "Put 'em up, Ben." Dickson stood still, smiled, then dropped the suitcases. As Dowling ordered again, "Come on, put 'em up," Ben darted under the partially open garage door. "I heard someone say 'Let him have it, he asked for it,'" Stella recalled. The officers stationed near the office starting firing, placing everyone else, including Stella and Musick, potentially in the line of fire. The officers emerging from the cabin near the two women hustled out of the way and moved the two women to a safer position. In about a minute, the officers fired at least forty-eight shots at Ben. Inside the garage, Ben struggled to start the cold Pontiac. On the first try, the car started, then stalled. While Ben struggled again with the cold engine, Shawnee County Deputy Sheriff Jack Beard fired two shots at the car's fuel tank. Topeka Detective Glenn Harris lobbed a tear-gas grenade toward the garage, but it landed short and unfavorable winds blew the gas back in the direction of the officers. The officers continued firing through the gap between the garage door and the ground. When he finally got the car running, Ben backed up, turning the rear of his car toward the office, destroying the garage door, scattering the officers who stood firing within twenty feet of the door, and plowing into the corner of the office building to the east, damaging the right side of his car. "I saw a man point a shotgun towards Johnny's head and I hollered 'Duck Johnny' and saw him duck down in the car as the man shot," Stella told the FBI.

Hunkered down and driving blind, Dickson put the car in a forward gear and sped away around the office and then south on Topeka Avenue. When the shooting started, the Kansas Highway Patrol officers had left their car on Topeka Avenue to join the fracas and were not in position to pursue Ben. The officers finally stopped firing as Ben sped away, and in the confusion Stella escaped into a nearby wooded area along Soldier Creek, pursued by a police officer. A few minutes later, Ben abandoned his car on Eugene Avenue just west of Topeka Avenue and north of the Kansas River, a little more than a mile south of the tourist camp. Photographs of the bullet-riddled car appeared in Topeka newspapers the next day. After abandoning the car, Ben stopped Mr. and Mrs. William Jensen, Iowans visiting friends in Topeka, and told them, "Get out of here, you'll get your car back pretty soon," and drove off in their late-model Dodge. The Jensens' car was found a few hours later near the Topeka Country Club at Twenty-Ninth Street and Burlingame Road. There was blood on the steering wheel. Ben then picked up the Buick he had left at the Redenbaugh home. Meanwhile, Stella tromped through the brush and weeds near the tourist camp, heading north along Soldier Creek, pursued by a police officer. Stella said in a statement to the FBI:

> I ducked into the bushes with my gun in my hand and the officer stopped about ten feet from me and didn't follow me any more. I kept on going. I ran as fast as I could and came to a bridge over a creek [one of several bridges crossing Soldier Creek north of the tourist camp]. I hid under that bridge the rest of the day and all night. The next morning, I walked to the highway and caught a ride with some fellows in a car.

During the night, Stella saw two men with rifles on the bridge searching for her. The men who picked Stella up drove her to a small town near Topeka where she and Ben had agreed to meet if they ever got separated. Stella told investigators she could not remember the name of the town.

When they reunited, Stella found that Ben had been injured in the melee. Two bullets had grazed his head, causing severe bleeding, and there were bullet holes in his clothes, including two holes in his scarf and several in his jacket. He may also have been hit in the shoulder. Police found a bullet hole in Dickson's hat, left behind on the front seat in the bullet-riddled car. On November 25, the *Topeka State Journal* reported that the car had bullet holes in the dashboard, in the seat cushion, and in the windshield, with the majority of the bullet holes on the passenger side of the car, indicating that many of the shots struck the car after Ben had backed out of the garage. In the suitcases Ben dropped, authorities found twenty-six rounds of ammunition, dozens of personal letters, several cryptic maps eventually identified as getaway routes for the Elkton and Brookings robberies, clothing, and other personal items. Those personal items, cataloged in the FBI files, again give a clue to what sort of person Dickson aspired to be and what kind of life Ben and Stella lived on the road. The contents included several books, including *Thus Spake Zarathustra* and *Beyond Good and Evil*, both by German poet and philosopher Friedrich Nietzsche. Ben, like many Americans in the 1930s, appears to have been drawn to the philosophy of Italian Fascist dictator Benito Mussolini, who was himself influenced by Nietzsche's writings. Among the items discovered in a car abandoned by the Dicksons in a St. Joseph, Missouri, garage a few days later was a newspaper clipping headlined "Boy Mussolini Dreamed of Becoming Super Man; Nietzsche's Broachings Cast Lasting Spell on Him." That same car contained a sheet of paper, apparently used for testing a typewriter, that began, "Mussolini — that prodigy of Nietsche [*sic*] is also a great leader of the Italian people." Apparently, Dickson had not allowed his studies to lapse.

In addition, the contents of the suitcases dropped in Topeka included a velvet pillow cover embroidered with "Souvenir of Windsor, Canada," no doubt collected during one of their visits to Detroit. There were other tourist trinkets and souvenirs in the suitcases as well.

That they kept letters from parents and friends indicates the loneliness of life on the road and suggests that they were thinking of family and friends and dreaming of a better future. The tourist trinkets suggest a headlong rush to find distractions to put the difficult and sometimes boring, sometimes frightening, fugitive life out of their minds. The suitcases were eventually turned over to the FBI but were found to have no evidentiary value.

Police arrested Musick, who was interviewed in her cell on November 28 by a *Topeka State Journal* reporter whose lurid report included descriptions of Musick's shapely legs and red lipstick. Musick said she met Stella at a roller-skating rink in 1937. "I went to Kansas City with Johnny and Estelle several times," Musick said. "We'd go to night clubs and shows and Johnny would pay the bills. Neither he nor Estelle ever took a drink. Johnny always had plenty of money, tho [*sic*] he didn't spend it foolishly. Most of it was in $1 bills." Ben was quiet, she said, and talked mostly about his plans to become a lawyer. While she never saw Ben with a gun, Musick said, Stella always carried a gun in her purse and had named it "Gertie."

For their trouble, the bumbling Topeka Police officers and Shawnee County Sheriff's deputies "captured" only the innocent Musick, two suitcases full of worthless evidence, and a bullet-riddled Pontiac. One of Ben's boxing friends later told the FBI that Topeka Police "hounded Ben for years" and that they could have captured him at the camp without firing a shot. The man told FBI investigators that "instead of one man walking up to him and quietly placing him under arrest, the Topeka Police Department sent a 'whole army' out to the place where Ben was with the intention of assassinating him." The man added that Ben was "one of the quickest thinkers in a crisis that he has ever seen." Hattie Redenbaugh's first husband, Raymond Baldwin, was also interviewed by FBI agents and said he had known Ben since he was a boy. Baldwin told an FBI agent that he would not cooperate with Topeka Police attempts to locate Ben, because they had "tried to slaughter Ben last Thanksgiving when they could have caught Ben and Estelle without shooting." Today, the actions of the police at the Ace Motor

Court would surely be judged reckless and excessive by most people. Although they were unaware of Ben's role in the South Dakota bank robberies and sought to arrest him only for the alleged Heidt assault and on suspicion of car theft, officers fired forty-eight shots at a man who did not return fire. Nevertheless, reports of the "shootout" at the Ace Motor Court, as it was called (despite the fact that only one side in the "shootout," the police, fired any shots), dramatically increased public interest in the Dickson case and became a crucial element in the FBI's efforts to prove that Dickson was a "vicious" outlaw. Bureau accounts and hundreds of news releases referred to the one-sided incident as a "gun battle" with authorities, an example of the sort of embellishments that routinely characterized news coverage of the Dicksons.

For Stella's mother and stepfather, news of the Ace Motor Court escape came as a shock. Before news reports identified their daughter's husband as Ben Dickson, they said they knew him only as Johnny O'Malley, which seems plausible given the relatively large population of Topeka and the age difference between Dickson and their daughter. On November 30, the *Topeka State Journal* reported, "The entire Redenbaugh family is completely aghast that the quiet-spoken, gentlemanly youth they knew as Johnny O'Malley, Chicago insurance man, is in reality Ben Dickson, who has served time in the Missouri penitentiary for bank robbery and the Kansas reformatory for highway robbery." Hattie Redenbaugh told the paper that Ben and Stella stayed with them whenever they were in Topeka, in all more than two of the seven months they had been together. Mrs. Redenbaugh noted that Ben never made any attempt to hide from police when they left the house and said she could not have asked for a better son-in-law. "He didn't drink and he didn't smoke," she said. "He didn't even use a profane word."

After the so-called shootout, the Dicksons traveled northeast, toward Detroit, taking side roads and avoiding the main highways. Ben's head injuries made it difficult for him to drive, because of headaches and dizziness, so Stella drove the car while her husband slept next to her in the front seat. Passing through Leonidas, Michigan, southeast of Kalamazoo on State Highway 60 just after midnight on November 28, 1938, four days after the escape from Topeka, Stella drove past a wrecked Ford car along the side of the road. Two Michigan State Patrol officers stood near the wreck, taking notes for an accident report. "I passed the wreck slowly because our motor was not working right and there were slow signs along the road," Stella said. "After I had passed the wreck a little ways, I noticed two highway patrolmen following us. They drove up near us and blew their sirens." After the Ace Motor Court incident, the Topeka Police, aware that Ben's car bore Michigan license plates, radioed police in Michigan and elsewhere to raise the alarm. The two Michigan State Patrol officers standing along the empty road had time as the Dickson car passed slowly to get a good look at the driver. As Stella struggled to get the malfunctioning Buick to pick up speed, Ben told her to keep going. "I told him the motor was not working properly, so he took the wheel," she recalled later. "He could not get the car to go any faster, so he started zigzagging."[1]

Despite the poor performance of the engine, the Dicksons eluded the patrolmen for three hours by driving with the headlights off on back roads. Several times they stopped and Dickson tried unsuccessfully to fix the faltering engine. Believing they had lost the officers, the Dicksons returned to the main highway, only to find themselves pursued again. This time, the officers began shooting at the Dickson car. It was the second time in four days that attempting to flee had prompted authorities to shoot at them. In this instance, though the officers may have suspected their identities, they fired ten shots despite a lack of confirmation. Dickson unzipped the back window of the cabriolet and ordered Stella to return fire. "Johnny told me to shoot low at the motor and tires, which I did," Stella told investigators. "Before I started shooting I was struck in the side of my head with either a bullet or a piece of metal that splintered off the car. I was bleeding badly and blood spurted all over Johnny." With her head bleeding and in the darkness and chaos of the moment, Stella was somehow able to disable the patrol car with only two shots. "I must have struck the patrol car because the car stopped," she recalled. The officers were uninjured and it was the only time during their time together as fugitives that either Ben or Stella fired a gun. The FBI referred to the incident as a "running gun battle" with police. In the same memorandum, the Special Agent in Charge (SAC) of the Bureau's Detroit office, John Bugas, noted that Ben "has not been considered dangerous." When he read the memorandum, Hoover drew a line through that sentence.

With the low-speed chase over, Ben and Stella knew they needed a new car. The engine of the Buick was already damaged before the chase and was working even more poorly afterward. At about three o'clock in the morning, they stopped at a farm nine miles southeast of Vicksburg, Michigan. Ben left the car running and knocked on the farmhouse door. An elderly man answered. Ben told the man he had run out of gas and needed to buy some fuel. The elderly man told Ben he was blind and would get his son, Claude Minnis, to help. When Minnis came out, he asked why, if Ben's car was out of gas, the car was still running. Ben pulled a revolver from his pocket and demanded that Minnis find him a car. Minnis tried unsuccessfully to start his 1928 Chevrolet. Giving up on the Chevy, Ben forced Minnis into the sputtering Buick and they drove to the nearby farm of Henry Metty. When they arrived, Minnis hollered for Metty to come to the door. When Metty emerged, Dickson pointed the revolver at him. Metty dressed quickly as he went out the door and shouted to his wife, "This man's got a gun and wants me to go with him." As he left the house, Metty tried awkwardly to punch Dickson, but the former boxer easily ducked the clumsy, roundhouse blow and Metty's fist struck the house instead. Dickson, still holding a gun but apparently unwilling to use it even when attacked, kept ducking blows until the much larger and slower Metty tired himself out. The two hostages transferred baggage from the Dicksons' car to Metty's 1934 Ford. Minnis and Metty were forced into the car, Minnis in back with Stella and Metty in front.

The personal items left in the car abandoned at Metty's farm again give hints about the Dicksons' travels and personalities. Among the items found in the car were two right-handed baseball gloves and a baseball, bathing suits, a UCLA Bruins poster, boxing gloves and shoes, a punching bag, four tennis balls, vacation pamphlets for Canadian and European destinations, course catalogs from UCLA, USC, and the University of Kansas, a "Liberty Songster Booklet," and thirty-nine books. Ben's books ranged from psychology textbooks to *The Complete Works of Homer* and *Karl Marx on Capital.* There were also several self-improvement booklets and a few detective magazines.

Ben told Metty to direct him to the Michigan-Indiana border. Stella said later:

> Mr. Metty directed us over the roads and I noticed that we went over the same bridge twice. Johnny noticed this too and we talked about it. Johnny told the farmer that if we got hurt they would get hurt too because the officers would shoot at the car not knowing that the farmers were in it. Following Mr. Metty's directions after we threatened him, we wound up on the same bridge a third time.

Finally arriving at the state line, Ben asked the farmers if they wanted to cross. Both said they did not. Ben told the men he needed them for a few more hours and offered to pay them for their trouble, apparently believing inaccurately that paying them somehow mitigated the act of hauling kidnapping victims across state lines. Stella told the FBI:

> [Ben] told them if they didn't go over the line with us willingly that the only thing he could do would be to leave them tied up to evade the Lindbergh kidnapping law. He told these farmers that we were young and had a long time to live and that our lives depended on our getting away. We also told them that the highway patrolmen had been chasing us and I showed them my head where I had been struck.

Metty and Minnis agreed to cross the state line in exchange for cash. Each man accepted fifteen dollars and Metty received an additional payment for the use of his car. Ben told them he wanted to get to a town where he could purchase another car. While trying to load her rifle in the backseat, Stella forgot to set the safety and accidently shot a hole in the convertible roof, startling everyone in the car, and shooting a hole in the FBI's theory that she was an expert with guns. During their drive to the state line, Ben was angry when he discovered that the Ford had a mechanical speed limiter that allowed a top speed of just forty-five miles per hour. "We wanted to stop someone on the highway and take their automobile so we kept watching faster cars," Stella said. Ben swerved the Ford several times, attempting to force an approaching car to stop. Eventually, he pulled over and parked the Ford on the shoulder to flag down a motorist. The man who stopped was Louis H. Karr, a salesman from South Bend, Indiana. Karr became the Dicksons' third hostage. Ben told Metty to drive the Ford with Stella holding him at gunpoint. Ben rode with Karr and Minnis in his Studebaker. After a few miles, they pulled over to transfer the baggage from the speed-limited Ford to the Studebaker. Ben asked Karr how much he earned in a day. Karr said he earned about six dollars. Ben paid Karr five dollars for the time he would lose and purchased Karr's hat for another five dollars. Now with three hostages and a new hat covering his bandaged head, Ben began driving toward Chicago.

"As we drove toward Chicago, Mr. Metty would wave at passing cars, trying to attract their attention," Stella said. "Johnny told Mr. Metty he would have to quit waving at passing cars or we would have to put him in the trunk. Metty kept on waving." Ben stopped the car, put a blanket in the trunk to cushion Metty's ride, and forced him in. Ben, fearing that his captive might suffocate from the car's exhaust, merely tied the trunk lid shut with rope, leaving a small gap for air. He told the farmer to pound on the trunk lid if the ride got too rough. A few miles later, Ben stopped the car at a railroad crossing fourteen miles from Valparaiso, Indiana. While they waited for the train to pass, Metty used a screwdriver he carried in his pocket to escape from the trunk. As he watched Metty lumber away through the fields, Ben decided the other hostages were too much trouble and released Karr and Minnis, paying them a few more dollars for inconveniencing them. They later reported that their captor had been a polite young man.

That same day, Ben was charged with a violation of the federal Dyer Act for the theft of the Buick from Kansas City in October. On

November 29, Ben and Stella were both charged with violations of the National Bank Robbery Act, specifically robbing FDIC-insured banks by taking hostages, in connection with the Elkton and Brookings robberies. Also on November 29, the two were charged with three federal counts of kidnapping in Detroit. The FBI office in Aberdeen, South Dakota, immediately began preparing information for wanted posters to be mailed to the Bureau's combined mailing list. Within a few days, six thousand wanted posters bearing photographs and descriptions of Ben and Stella had been mailed to libraries, post offices, and police and sheriff's offices nationwide. Before November 28, Ben Dickson was only wanted in Topeka for state charges following the assault on Irl Heidt and in Missouri for a parole violation. The next day, the Dicksons were the FBI's Public Enemies No. 1 and No. 2.

On November 29, the FBI was contacted, apparently by a former Missouri penitentiary inmate living in St. Louis who claimed to have been visited by Ben and Stella in September. The man promised to contact the FBI should the Dicksons return. Bureau Assistant Director Edward A. Tamm wrote a note on a teletype from St. Louis SAC Gerald B. Norris. "I instructed St. Louis to watch this very closely." By the beginning of December, the Bureau was in contact with one of the people who would later lead Ben into a trap.

In addition to the initiation of an extensive investigation to find the Dicksons, the FBI also ramped up its public relations machinery to publicize the case. Ben and Stella Mae Dickson fit perfectly into the Bureau's public relations template. Ben was a charismatic and handsome bank robber like Dillinger, and the Dicksons were a married couple like Bonnie Parker and Clyde Barrow. They had roamed across the Midwest like the outlaws of earlier in the decade and there was no telling what could happen next. Of course, Dillinger, Barrow, and Parker were, unlike the Dicksons, "vicious" and violent criminals who were involved in multiple murders, including the killing of several enforcement officers and FBI agents. No innocents were injured during the Dicksons' crime spree. Like Bonnie Parker, Stella Mae Dickson was portrayed in the media as a gun moll, in part because FBI public relations releases presented her as such. For the FBI, handsome boxer Ben and pretty "gun moll" Stella were perfect props for a public relations campaign. Between December 1, 1938, and the end of April 1939, FBI Crime Records agents distributed thousands of press releases and tens of thousands of wanted posters across the country.

Probably unaware that they had been identified as fugitives by the FBI, Ben and Stella drove from Valparaiso, Indiana, to Calumet City, Illinois, where they stowed the stolen car. Then they drove to Hammond, Indiana, where they rented a room in a house and stayed for two days. In Hammond, they watched the newspapers for an opportunity to buy a car, noting that Metty, Minnis, and Karr had told their story to police and to newspaper reporters and undoubtedly discovering that they were sought by the FBI. Apparently seeking new license plates to avoid identification, Ben purchased a worn-out Model A Ford for forty dollars and they drove south, stashed the Model A in a rented garage, and bought a newer Ford. During their trip, they were sighted in Excelsior Springs, Missouri, a resort town about thirty miles northeast of Kansas City. At about 7:30 a.m. on November 30, 1938, Matt Kennell, an employee of Dr. Ball's Bath House, noticed a black Ford V8 coach parked in the driveway in front of the bathhouse. Kennell, a valet, went to the curb and opened the driver's side door. Inside he saw a young woman in the driver's seat and a man with several days' growth of beard reclining in the backseat, propped up and seeming to favor one shoulder. Kennell noticed bandages on the man's head and shoulder and saw that he was pale and sickly looking. Stella immediately put the car in reverse, backed out of the driveway, and drove away. The Excelsior Springs incident was the last confirmed public sighting of the Dicksons in 1938.

For the rest of 1938 and the first weeks of 1939, the FBI had no idea where the fugitives might be hiding. Bureau reports for that period include efforts to verify unconfirmed sightings, laboratory reports on items found in the couple's abandoned cars, and very little solid information about where they might have gone. Bureau officials moved additional agents from Dallas to the Lake Benton area, assuming that Ben and Stella might return to the cabin or the Johnson farm near Tyler. Agents spoke again with James Dickson in Topeka, urging him to turn in his son should he return. James Dickson said he would not turn them in but would advise them to surrender themselves. "Subject's father James D. Dickson, Topeka, is so uncooperative and has reputation for several years of protecting subject in every way possible and will aid him in any manner," Kansas City SAC Guinane told Hoover in a teletype. Agents returned to reinterview James and Darwin Dickson on December 16, 1938, specifically confronting "Professor Dickson" with evidence that he had assisted his fugitive son. "Professor Dickson went to great lengths to explain that Ben's conviction and sentence to the Kansas State Reformatory was the result of a frameup and untruthful testimony," Guinane wrote. "The Professor's mind seems to be imbued with two things only, i.e., chemistry and a desire to protect Ben." Hattie Redenbaugh, Guinane reported, "has a poor reputation with [local] police" and was unlikely to assist the investigation.

Tens of thousands of additional wanted circulars were printed and distributed in Kansas City, Detroit, Chicago, Topeka, Omaha, Des Moines, and elsewhere. Alleged sightings of the Dicksons were reported in Milwaukee, Indianapolis, Omaha, and even Atlanta, Baltimore, and Philadelphia. Even Hoover seemed confused by the widely scattered "sightings" prompted by the Bureau's thousands of circulars and hundreds of news releases. When a news clipping from the *Baltimore Sun* headlined "Dickson Pair Reported in Baltimore" came across his desk, Hoover scrawled a note on the clipping: "Just what are the facts about this?" An FBI assistant director checked out the "sighting" and reported to Hoover, in a three-page memorandum, that it was based on a public report that turned out to be false and was then embellished by a creative reporter.

Those false sightings notwithstanding, a few days later, Crime Records chief Nichols mailed out a new round of press releases and photographs of Ben and Stella to reporters and editors nationwide. "I feel that widespread publicity on the activities of this pair of desperadoes will be very helpful in focusing public attention on them, and will

possibly result in our receiving information as to their whereabouts,"
Nichols wrote in a letter signed by Hoover and distributed to more
than four hundred journalists nationwide who were included on the
Bureau's Special Correspondents List of "friendly" reporters, editors,
radio news reporters, and publishers. The nationwide scope of the mailing confirmed the fact that the FBI had no idea where the Dicksons
had gone and, at least insofar as public relations was concerned, did not
care. Journalist friends of the FBI immediately responded, publishing
stories like the one that appeared on the front page of the *Boston Daily
Record* on January 20, 1939, next to Stella's picture, claiming that the
Dicksons had been spotted near there. To add local flavor, the Boston
reporter embellished his story by claiming that fifty FBI agents were
"trailing" Dickson and had traced them to Nashua, New Hampshire,
the night before. The local SAC was forced to write a memorandum
for Hoover pointing out that the reporter had made up that claim.
On the same day it was reported that the Dicksons were in Boston,
the *Dallas Dispatch-Journal* reported that a "Southwest Search for New
Desperado Couple Revives Memories of Clyde, Bonnie." Similar stories, many of them with fictional "local" angles, began appearing in
newspapers across the country. In a February 2, 1939, memorandum,
Nichols reported to Hoover that the news releases had been "sent to
the entire United States."

The Bureau had begun referring to Ben and Stella as Public Enemies
No. 1 and No. 2 immediately after they were charged with kidnapping
and bank robbery in late November 1938. By December, the Dicksons
had discovered from newspaper coverage that they had become nationally sought fugitives, and with the FBI in pursuit, the couple concocted
a plan to confuse authorities and buy time. On December 2, 1938, en
route to New Orleans, Stella wrote a letter to her mother. The letter,
postmarked at Taylorville, Illinois, began, "Dear Mom, do not get ex-
cited when I tell you this." The letter continued with a bogus story of
Ben's death from injuries he received at the Ace tourist camp. Ben had
begun to develop a fever shortly after the Ace Motor Court shooting
and died, Stella claimed in the letter:

So I drove down close to the [Missouri] River and buried him. I dug as good a grave as I could with the tools and covered it with brush and stuff as good as I could. I put his gun and all his clothes and things over him like he told me to. The sun started to come up before I got thru and I saw it was quite a ways from the river. I'm going back to see some friends of ours in Michigan and take up dance and singing. They offered me a job the last time we were there. Tell Johnnies [*sic*] folks I'll try to see them when I can. Say hello to Jr and to Dad. Goodbye and don't worry.

Stella mailed the letter to a school friend who called Hattie Redenbaugh and delivered it to her. Mrs. Redenbaugh then showed the letter to an attorney and he advised her to turn it over to the FBI.

The FBI knew from reports of witnesses to the Topeka shooting, from the bloodied Jensen car, and from the Excelsior Springs sighting that Ben had been wounded at the Ace Motor Court, so Stella's report was deemed plausible. Several unlucky agents were dispatched to the Taylorville area to search along the banks of the Missouri River for a shallow grave. For more than a month, agents tromped up and down the riverbanks with no success. Agents searched near bridges at Taylorville, Breckenridge, Beardstown, Meredosia, Florence, Havan, and Alton in Illinois. Another team of agents searched near the same bridges on the other side of the river. Given Stella's small stature, weighing only about 110 pounds, it seems unlikely, even had Ben died of his injuries, that she would have been able to drag his body from the car to the banks of the river and then bury him in a grave she had dug herself. On January 5, 1939, in a memorandum to Investigative Division Chief Edward Allen Tamm, one of the agents searching the riverbanks pointed out reports that both Dicksons had allegedly been sighted in Iowa on December 8, 1938, six days after the date on Stella's letter. The unconfirmed sighting, according to the agent, suggested that they were wasting their time searching the banks of the Missouri River. "While the above information is of no value in the investigation to locate these fugitives, it is of some interest in that it indicates the information relative to Ben Dickson's death is not correct." FBI Director J. Edgar Hoover, who read investigative memoranda related to major cases, underlined "not correct" on the memo. Bureau news releases sent to reporters nationwide on January 13, 1939, do not mention the Taylorville letter, suggesting that the FBI had by then concluded that reports of Ben's death were false. Still, his injuries were thought to be serious enough that the couple's visit to Excelsior Springs was perceived as an indication that they were seeking medical treatment. Tens of thousands of additional wanted circulars were sent to doctors in areas thought to be potential destinations for Ben and Stella. In addition to their usual mailing list of government offices and police departments, the Bureau eventually sent wanted posters to tourist camp owners, boxing promoters, gas station owners, and pharmacists across the country.

While Ben and Stella's ruse had failed to shut down the manhunt, it had forced the FBI to expend significant investigative manpower on a futile search along the banks of the Missouri River far from the couple's actual destination. Meanwhile, the Dicksons arrived in New Orleans in December, moving in together as Mr. and Mrs. Robert Kane in a rented room at 2409 St. Charles Avenue. They stayed there for three weeks before moving to their last home together, five-room apartment number 3 at 615 Exposition Boulevard across from Audubon Park. For thirty-two dollars a month, they rented the apartment, again under the alias of Mr. and Mrs. Robert Kane. Their landlord told the FBI that the couple rarely emerged during the daytime except to play tennis or to hit golf balls at a driving range nearby. When they went out, according to the landlord, it was usually in the late afternoon and they usually did not return until four o'clock in the morning or later. They spent evenings attending motion pictures and visiting nightclubs. "We went a few times to the Cat and the Fiddle, the Little Forest, Tyler's Garden in Audubon Park, and we also went to moving pictures a great deal," Stella told the FBI. She said the couple also took a ride in a plane over the city and Ben briefly considered the possibility of taking pilot lessons and using a plane to escape after small-town robberies but gave up the idea when he discovered it would cost him more than $600 to earn a pilot's license. Bureau agents found a Truetone radio in the apartment, Mardi Gras souvenirs, many magazines, and fishing equipment. There were numerous receipts for milk delivery dated from January 14 to April 1, no doubt for Ben, who did not drink coffee.

Ben continued shuffling cars in an apparent attempt to shield the couple's trail from authorities. They bought a new Chrysler, which they kept for a few weeks before trading it in for a new Ford. Stella later told the FBI that Ben tried to continue his education, using aliases obtained through their classified advertisement scheme. Both Ben and Stella registered for courses at a local community college and Ben sought admission to Tulane University. At one point, neighbors recalled, Ben collected the mail, opened and read a letter, tore it up, and angrily kicked leaves over it. It seems at least possible that the letter was a rejection of his application for admission to Tulane. Nevertheless, Ben appears to have continued his studies at a community college and informally on his own, probably under the long-distance, pen-pal tutelage of his father. Earlier stashes uncovered by the FBI included letters from Dickson's father, James, that indicated he was still directing Ben's studies by suggesting and even sending him books. Among the books found in the Dicksons' New Orleans apartment were *Capital*, by Karl Marx, *The Complete Poems of Keats and Shelley*, *Outline of History*, by H. G. Wells, and *Mein Kampf*, by Adolf Hitler. Ironically, the book collection also included *Ten Thousand Public Enemies*, by Hoover's frequent public relations collaborator, journalist Courtney Ryley Cooper. Cooper was Hoover's most frequent public relations collaborator between 1935 and 1940, ghostwriting more than twenty articles for the FBI director. In *Ten Thousand Public Enemies*, the former circus clown Cooper asserted that America was infested with criminals, ordinary people who were hiding in plain sight. Hoover authored the foreword for the book. Cooper committed suicide in 1940 shortly after Hoover cut him off from FBI information and ended their collaboration when an article Cooper ghostwrote for him outlining the dangers of tourist camps as criminal hideouts sparked an outcry from tourist camp owners nationwide.

In addition to the books, the Dicksons' New Orleans apartment held several pages of Ben's original writings. As in previous caches located by the FBI, the writings offered insight into Ben's discipline. Only brief descriptions of the pages exist in FBI files. One page began, "Since it is to my benefit to write one hour a day I shall try to improve each day in composition and penmanship." In New Orleans, Ben also stashed sixteen sticks of dynamite, prompting later speculation that he had one time planned to break Pretty Boy Floyd associate Adam Richetti out of the Missouri State Penitentiary. While there is no factual indication of what Ben planned to do with the dynamite, the rumors of a Missouri breakout plan appear unfounded, since Richetti was executed in the gas chamber on October 7, 1938, seven months before the dynamite was found in the apartment. Bureau files contain little information other than acknowledging rumors about the plot and an unconfirmed report that, sometime in October, the Dicksons moved into a home in Jefferson City near the penitentiary. When one agent did investigate the possibility that Ben had plotted a Missouri prison break, he concluded, "It did not appear at the present time that there was any one in the institution with whom Dickson was sufficiently interested to go to this trouble and risk to attempt to liberate."

For six months before the location of Ben Dickson in St. Louis on April 6, 1939, the FBI had been hunting, and failing to find any sign of, the fugitive couple. In November 1938, FBI Assistant Director Edward A. Tamm sent a teletype message to Guinane and his fifty-one other SACs around the country, urging them to make the Dickson case their top priority. "I told Mr. Guinane to bear down on the case and carry out every available lead at once," Tamm wrote in a November 28, 1938, memorandum. "I stated that the director [J. Edgar Hoover] wants it given preferred and immediate attention." Another teletype, this one from Hoover, was sent to SACs in South Dakota, Nebraska, Minnesota, Wisconsin, Illinois, Iowa, Michigan, and Indiana on the next day, ordering that the case be given "preferred, expeditious and immediate investigative attention." Hoover further ordered those offices to remain open twenty-four hours a day, seven days a week, until the Dicksons were found. Finally, in the teletype Hoover authorized a payment of $5,000 (the equivalent of $85,000 in 2015) to informants in the case who provided information leading to an arrest. With no idea where Ben and Stella might be hiding, the Bureau issued press releases nationwide suggesting that people in those localities be on the lookout for Public Enemies No. 1 and No. 2. The press releases triggered another flurry of stories, from Maine to California, claiming, falsely, that the Dicksons had been sighted in those locations. Those stories, based only on a generic FBI press release urging people to watch out for the fugitives, demonstrate how newspaper reporters and editors were willing to add sensational details to FBI news to localize Bureau exploits. They also demonstrate the power of the FBI to shape the public conversation about crime and criminals.

6

ST. LOUIS

While Ben and Stella settled into a relatively normal life in New Orleans, the FBI was catching up to them. Interviews with Ben's prison associates, prompted by potential cash rewards, provided important clues for authorities. On December 13, 1938, the Bureau received word that a car belonging to the Dicksons was found in a rented garage in St. Joseph, Missouri. The 1936 Ford was left in the garage on November 11, 1938. Witnesses said Ben dropped the car off, paid three dollars for one month's rent, and left in a taxi. Ben and Stella returned on November 21 and again on November 27, shortly after the Ace Motor Court shootout, to remove property from the car and paid another three months' rent on the garage. The garage owner contacted local police after reading in his local newspaper about the Dicksons being sighted at Excelsior Springs.

When agents entered the garage on December 15, they found the Ford in poor condition with a cracked windshield and dented fender. A University of California, Los Angeles sticker adorned the rear window. A few fingerprints were lifted from the car but were of poor quality and proved to be of no use in identifying the source. Inside the car, agents found another cache of personal memorabilia. The personal items again suggested the couple's continued attempts to maintain contact with friends and family even as they zigzagged across the Midwest. There were letters from family, items indicating that Ben continued to attempt to advance his education, and trinkets from tourist attractions. Many of the letters in the car were excerpted in FBI files, but none were kept intact. Many of the items relate to Ben's education. One scrap of lined paper bore class schedule notations. The list began with "Magazine Article Writing, M.W., 8-9," and ended with "Current Events, 7-9." A class-listing brochure, "Opportunity," published by the Manual Arts Adult Evening School in Los Angeles, was left in the car. Several classes in the evening school brochure were highlighted with a red pencil, including Arts and Crafts, Flower Making, Business Law, Business English, Beginning Diction and Theory, Beginning Radio Speech, and Advanced Radio Speech.

The agents who examined the car reported that the interior was a mess, with items ranging from popcorn and puffed wheat to receipts and letters littering the floorboards. Among the other items found in the car were copies of *Liberty* magazine, a popular general interest periodical that branded itself the "weekly for everybody." A few months later, *Liberty*'s April issue included a highly fictionalized feature about "gun moll" Stella Mae Dickson. Agents could also tell from the items left in the car that Stella had been indulging her love of singing. Several copies of *Song Hits*, a magazine that printed lyrics to popular songs of the time, were found in the car. Stella was also trying to disguise her identity by changing her appearance. In the backseat, agents found a mat of brown or light brown hair that "was probably cut from a woman's head." None of the recovered items led directly to their location. Once again, though, the items provide insight into the Dicksons' day-to-day life on the road. Even after both of them had been shot, they were desperately trying to find a way to live a normal life and improve themselves, striving for, as Ben wrote in one of his amateur poems, "something higher." Ben continued his studies. Stella indulged her teenage love of popular songs and tried a new hairstyle. They sang songs. They visited tourist destinations. The relatively normal life they made for themselves for several months in New Orleans must have been a tremendous relief for them.

Ben and Stella likely spent the Christmas and New Year's holidays in New Orleans. Stella later told a friend and neighbor that she and Ben had enjoyed a special meal together on New Year's Eve in 1938. In Topeka, FBI agents again visited James Dickson's home and interviewed him. Professor Dickson told them he had a miserable Christmas. Dickson told the agents that he spent the holiday worrying about harm befalling his son. "It certainly was a poor Christmas around here and I'm glad it's over," Dickson told the agents.

After the car was recovered in St. Joseph, FBI investigators turned their full attention to Ben's acquaintances from his years behind The Walls in Jefferson City. Beginning in late 1938, with the authorization of up to a $5,000 payment for clues that led to the Dicksons' arrest, agents began contacting former Missouri inmates hoping to find someone Ben maintained contact with. The FBI described that search in a news release produced after the case was concluded. "Investigation was also conducted relative to various criminal associates of Ben Dickson, principally persons with whom he had been confined to the Missouri State Penitentiary, and it was through this investigation that accurate information was obtained to indicate that the Dicksons had traveled to St. Louis Missouri on February 13, 1939." The first interviews with Dickson's prison friends took place in late 1938 and continued during the first three months of 1939. After each interview, the subjects were told first about penalties under the federal harboring of fugitives law and then were told about the $2,500 reward for information leading to the capture of each of the Dicksons, a total of $5,000. One of the men interviewed in Kansas City urged agents to speak to Dickson's prison friend Whitey Kyle and to a man identified in FBI files only as "Curtis," both of whom lived in St. Louis.[1]

In fact, Ben had remained in touch with both Whitey and Curtis, and the Dicksons had stayed in St. Louis for several days in early 1939.

The lure of a $5,000 reward proved too much to resist for one of his friends. Stella described the events of February 13 in her April interview with FBI agents. "Not long ago Johnny and I were in St. Louis and Johnny wanted to get in touch with a friend of his named Whitey Kyle. I understood that Johnny and Kyle were in the penitentiary at Jefferson City together. Johnny also knew a person in St. Louis named Curtis, who was Johnny's best friend," Stella said. The origins of Ben's friendship with Curtis is unclear in the files. There were no students named Curtis in Ben's class at school, so it seems more likely that Curtis was a friend from the amateur boxing ranks. Stella continued:

> Johnny wanted to get some money to a girl in St. Louis who was the sister of [another prison] friend Walt. The girl's name was Naomi and she was a nurse. On that occasion in St. Louis Johnny drove near Curtis's home and I got out of the car and saw a little girl coming from a grocery store. I put $50 with a loaf of bread in the sack and paid the little girl to take the money and the bread to Curtis's home.

Witnesses interviewed by the FBI remembered the story slightly differently. The clerk of a Dobbins Grocery Store on North Spring Avenue recalled that a young woman he identified from a photograph as Stella visited the store at about 6:30 p.m. on February 13, purchased a bag of White Cross Egg Noodles (spelled "Nudles" in the FBI file), a loaf of white bread, and a package of Wheaties cereal for 27 cents. The young girls Stella spoke to told FBI agents that a woman approached them near the corner of North Vandeventer and Market Street, about four blocks from Dobbins Store, and asked them to take the groceries and an envelope, later discovered to contain a note and thirty-five dollars in cash, to a nearby apartment. Stella gave the girls 10 cents to complete the errand. The idea was that Curtis would act as a go-between, making sure Naomi got the money, which was apparently intended to help pay medical bills for Naomi and Walt's mother. The envelope included with the groceries was just the first payment to Naomi. The note (the contents of which were, inexplicably, completely redacted in FBI files) said Ben planned to return to St. Louis after a few weeks with more money for Naomi and Walt's mother.

The exact circumstances under which the FBI discovered that the Dicksons would return to St. Louis on April 6, 1939, are unclear because of exhaustive redactions in that portion of the Dickson FBI file. In fact, very little of the narrative of the Dickson case between February through April 1939 remains unredacted. The redactions, under the privacy and investigative procedures exemptions in the Freedom of Information and Privacy Act, have obscured the details, but the general means by which the Dicksons were tracked to St. Louis are discernible. The FBI learned of the February 13 visit, the thirty-five dollars for Naomi, and the note to Curtis the evening they were delivered. Given events that followed, and reading between the lines of the redacted file, it seems very likely that Curtis, in hopes of collecting the reward, contacted the FBI on February 13 and put agents in touch with Naomi.

Naomi would become the key to catching Ben. After she was contacted by the FBI, Naomi became an FBI informant, no doubt acting under the promise of a potential $5,000 reward. The FBI's trap was set for the next time Ben contacted Naomi to set up a meeting to give her money for her mother's care. Naomi was instructed to call St. Louis FBI SAC Gerald B. Norris whenever she next heard from Ben. Just three weeks later, on April 4, 1939, Ben and Stella again left New Orleans heading for St. Louis. They stayed in a tourist camp on April 4 and at a Cape Girardeau, Missouri, rooming house on April 6. They arrived in St. Louis at about 6:30 p.m. on April 6, 1939. When they arrived, Stella called Naomi from a pay phone and arranged for Ben to meet her at 7:00 p.m. at the Yankee System Hamburger Shop on 16 South Euclid Avenue, just east of Forest Park and near the hospital where Naomi worked. The meeting was not previously planned but instead was initiated that evening by Ben, who likely had Stella make the call in case the FBI had wiretapped Naomi's telephone.

The sidewalks in midtown St. Louis near Forest Park were bustling with people on the warm spring evening of Friday, April 6, 1939. The neighborhood included two major luxury hotels, two large hospitals,

Gerald B. Norris, special agent in charge of the St. Louis office of the FBI, led the team of four agents who staked out the Yankee System Hamburger Shop on April 6, 1939. (Courtesy of the National Archives at College Park, Record Group 65HN, #2529.)

and many small shops and restaurants in addition to the nearby Forest Park. Thanks to the good weather, the South Euclid Avenue area was a hub of activity. The Dicksons arrived in the neighborhood just before 7:00 p.m. Ben, dressed in gray pants, a light blue shirt and blue tie, a gray hat, and a blue plaid lumber jacket, parked their car on the west side of Euclid Avenue about one block south of intersecting Laclede

Avenue. The east side of the street included several restaurants and shops. The Yankee System Hamburger Shop at 16 South Euclid Avenue occupied the south half of the first building north of an alley on the east side of the street. The front of the hamburger shop featured a modern, light-colored facade with the colorful lettering "Yankee System" above the door and "5¢ Hamburgers 5¢" vertically to the left of the entrance. The glass door was framed by a large, angled window on either side. Like many storefront buildings of the same vintage, the shop occupied one-third of the building, a larger shop occupied the north portion, and the two shops were separated by a door leading up to apartments on the second floor. That door was situated about ten feet north of the Yankee System front door.

Ben was scheduled to meet with Naomi in the shop at 7:00 p.m. He was heavily armed, with two revolvers stuffed in the waistband of his pants under his jacket and a knife concealed in his pocket. Stella waited in the car. According to witnesses, Naomi arrived first, entered, and, not seeing Ben, left before returning a few minutes later. She sat at the counter near the front window and waited for Ben to arrive. She was dressed in dark, possibly brown, clothing with a stylish black hat that nearly covered her eyes. In one of the tables along the left-hand wall of the shop sat an FBI agent, sipping coffee and eating a sandwich. The twenty-three-year-old waitress working that day, Gloria Cameron, would prove a key witness to events that evening. In addition to the agent inside, three more agents waited in a barbershop across the street to the west, led by SAC Norris. In hopes of collecting the $5,000 reward, Naomi had agreed to call Norris when she heard from Ben and had telephoned him at 6:45 p.m. By coincidence, the Yankee System Hamburger Shop was just a few blocks from Norris's apartment and he contacted the only available special agents from the St. Louis FBI office, Edward Louis Cochran, Pierce Pratt, and John Bush, and met them at the barbershop across the street from the hamburger shop.[2]

Statements by Norris and officials in the Bureau's public relations–oriented Crime Records Section would later deny that Naomi existed or that any paid informant had led them to Ben. They would instead claim that detective work had cracked the case, a more heroic version of events. Oddly enough, they could well have claimed truthfully that detective work led them to Naomi, but for some reason (perhaps by her request or for her safety) they left her out of the story. Nevertheless, Naomi came to be known in newspaper accounts of the evening as "the woman in black" or "woman in brown," an homage to Anna Sage, the "woman in red," who led FBI agents to Dillinger at the Biograph Theater in Chicago in 1934 and collected an FBI reward before being deported. The erasure of Naomi from Bureau accounts of the case was but one of many significant discrepancies in FBI accounts of the evening. Bureau documents, however, confirm that Naomi was eventually paid $2,500 for her assistance in locating Ben.

When the special agent inside the shop was unable to positively identify the fugitive, he left the shop, went across the street, and informed Norris. Norris himself twice walked past the window of the shop, peering in at Ben, seated with Naomi at the counter four feet from the window. Convinced that the man in the shop was Ben, Norris and the other three agents huddled in the alley just out of sight of the Yankee System front windows to hatch a plan. Concerned that passersby on the street might be endangered if they simply waited for Dickson to leave, the agents decided to enter the shop, grab Dickson, pin his arms, and drag him out the back door. While the agents were hatching that sensible plan, however, the woman and then Ben exited the shop. When he came out, the four agents were clustered in the alley south of the shop, facing generally north toward the door with Norris and Bush in front and Cochran and Pratt behind. Norris identified himself as a federal agent and ordered Ben to surrender.

Differing accounts of what happened next can be found in newspaper and FBI file sources. The various accounts are significant in part because of what they show about the FBI's institutional culture and because they indicate that the actual circumstances were kept from the public in order to avoid negative publicity for the Bureau. Two different accounts of the few seconds following Norris's order to surrender can be found in FBI records, the first of which was discarded in favor of the second, largely fictional version, which was less likely to prove an embarrassment to the Bureau. A third account of the shooting, a more credible version in many ways, was provided by the only citizen witness who stepped forward, twenty-three-year-old Yankee System waitress Gloria Cameron.

The FBI claimed in its statements to reporters that Dickson emerged from the shop and, when ordered to surrender, crouched and either reached for or pulled a gun, prompting all four of the agents, their lives in danger, to shoot and kill him. Dickson was struck twice and died on the sidewalk. Questioned by a *St. Louis Post-Dispatch* reporter that evening, Norris claimed that each agent fired one shot, an effort to avoid admitting that only one agent, Bush, fired his gun. The killing was justified, according to FBI statements, as an act of self-defense by federal agents who feared for their lives. The FBI's public version of the story, often embellished even further, has survived the decades, appearing in books and radio scripts written or approved by Bureau publicists. One of the agents at the scene, Cochran, recounted the tale in his 1966 memoirs, *FBI Man*. It appears highly likely that the truth of the event was very different from those and other FBI-endorsed versions of the shooting. There were several key discrepancies. First, the Bureau denied that any informant was involved in their efforts to locate Dickson that night. Gloria Cameron, in statements to reporters, confirmed that Dickson had met a "woman in black," wearing a distinctive hat that covered her eyes, in the shop that night. Norris claimed that agents had been called to the scene by a call from an anonymous man and that he knew nothing of a woman informant. Most importantly, Cameron's recollection of the shooting itself did not match the FBI's public version.

According to Cameron, Naomi left the shop ahead of Ben and then, after they both reached the sidewalk outside, she turned and quickly reentered, taking the same seat she had occupied a few seconds earlier. Standing alone on the sidewalk, Ben was confronted by Norris and Bush, who moved toward the shop from the alley with the two other agents behind them. According to Cameron, Ben did not reach for his guns.

Instead, he turned his back to the approaching agents and attempted to open the apartment door about ten feet north of the exit door of the hamburger shop. According to Cameron, quoted in an April 7, 1939, *St. Louis Post-Dispatch* story, it was as Ben struggled in vain to open the locked door to escape up the stairs that he was struck by two bullets and fell right in front of the apartment door. "Two men stepped up to Dickson and he turned and started to run north," she said. "Then there were two shots and Dickson fell." Cameron then saw one of the agents lean over Dickson's body, pull out a piece of paper, and "grin sort of satisfied and put it in his pocket." One of the agents entered the shop to ask Naomi, "Is that the right man?" She nodded and then was whisked away in the agent's personal car, sobbing. Another witness, Clarence Kingston, told the *Post-Dispatch* he did not see the shooting but turned and saw Dickson on the pavement. "I heard him groan, 'Oh, my God,' then let out a terrible scream." Another citizen witness, John Hayes, recorded as a "Negro porter," who happened to be in the barbershop across the street, was looking out the window, heard the shots, and saw Dickson fall. St. Louis police did not interview Kingston or Hayes. A photograph in the *St. Louis Post-Dispatch* on April 7 showed a man pointing to the spot on the ground where Dickson's body was found. He is pointing to the ground directly in front of the apartment door, ten or twelve feet north of the hamburger shop exit.

Information in internal FBI reports of the incident corroborate much of Cameron's version of the story. In a so-called Personal and Confidential letter to J. Edgar Hoover, Norris recounted the shooting and described Dickson's wounds. "Agent [name redacted, probably John Bush] shot him twice in the body, *one bullet entering his shoulder and going down through his body toward the front* and the other *going from one side of his body to the other* [emphasis added]." The bullet that struck Dickson in his side, according to FBI reports, entered under his right arm and also passed toward the front of his body. If, as Bureau accounts claimed, Dickson was directly in front of and facing the agents, reaching for or drawing his gun, it would seem impossible for bullets to travel in a trajectory from the back to the front of his body. In addition, if Dickson had been crouching and reaching for his gun or brandishing it, it is hard to imagine how he was shot *under* his right arm with a back-to-front trajectory by agents standing and approaching him. If, however, Dickson had turned his right side to the agents approaching from the south and attempted to open the apartment door north of the shop's exit, as Cameron recalled, he would have been turned in such a way that the agent who fired, approaching from the south, might have fired bullets that followed the generally back-to-front, right side–to–left side trajectories. As to whether Dickson was actually threatening the agents, there was no claim that he managed to pull out a weapon but rather he "went for" his guns. Norris told Hoover in a letter that he grabbed the dying man's hands as he lay on the pavement to assure that he could not pull out a gun and then found both guns in the waistband of Ben's pants. Norris said he felt Dickson's hands relax as he died on the sidewalk.

The fact that only one agent fired his weapon is also telling. It is difficult to imagine that three of four highly trained FBI agents, their guns drawn, would have withheld fire had they actually been approaching an armed man who was threatening them. The only account that seems credible came from the only unbiased witness, Cameron. It is worth remembering that Ben had, when confronted by armed police in Topeka in November 1938, turned and run, a precedent for the escape attempt described by Cameron. It appears highly likely that Dickson was shot by one overzealous agent as he attempted to escape. The facts of the shooting were sufficiently unclear that, on the orders of the St. Louis County coroner, two FBI agents were placed on what was described as "technical arrest" after the shooting by St. Louis Police Department officers. Unfortunately, St. Louis Police Department records of the shooting have been lost. Only an index card indicating that Dickson "was shot and killed by FBI agents here" remains. Darwin Dickson later claimed that his brother-in-law, a St. Louis carpenter, John Pitman, by chance witnessed the shooting and confirmed that Ben was shot with his left hand on the doorknob and right hand higher on the door, a notion that seems consistent with the back-to-front bullet wound under his right arm.

Norris's handling of the shooting with his superiors in Washington also indicates that the Bureau wanted to clean up its public account of the incident to make it more heroic. When St. Louis Police Department officers arrived on the scene, placed two (unnamed) FBI agents under "technical arrest," and attempted to question the FBI agents, Norris refused to be interviewed and refused to allow the other agents to speak to local law enforcement officers. "All of this information [about the shooting]," Norris wrote to Hoover in his "personal and confidential" letter, "was furnished to the bureau before it was given out to any other sources." It is difficult to imagine why, if the shooting was proper and in self-defense, Norris would simply refuse to speak to local police officers doing their duty to investigate the killing. Before making any statements to police or the press, Norris wanted to confer with his superiors in Washington. The contents of those discussions, with the assistant director in charge of the Investigative Division, Edward Allen Tamm, further indicate that the Bureau was laboring to sanitize the story of the shooting to avoid embarrassment.

A St. Paul, Minnesota, native, Tamm joined the FBI in 1930 after graduating with a law degree from Georgetown University. Tamm rose quickly through the ranks and in 1938 was put in charge of the Investigative Division, which oversaw the law enforcement and investigatory work of all field agents. He left the Bureau in 1948 to accept President Harry S. Truman's appointment as a federal judge in Washington. In 1965, President Lyndon B. Johnson named him to the nation's most important federal appellate court, the Court of Appeals for the District of Columbia Circuit, a position he held until his death in 1986. Hoover, who took personally Tamm's decision to leave the Bureau in 1948, placed his former aide on the FBI's "do not contact" list. In 1969, when Tamm was considered by President Richard M. Nixon for an opening on the US Supreme Court, Hoover maneuvered through Justice Department officials to have Tamm removed from consideration.

Among Tamm's duties in 1938 was the oversight of all investigative activities of the FBI. Thus, it was Tamm whom Norris called immediately following the Dickson shooting and then several more times the next day. The substance of their initial conversation was summarized

FBI Assistant Director Edward Allen Tamm worked with SAC Gerald B. Norris in the hours after the shooting of Ben Dickson to craft a narrative that covered up the actual nature of the shooting. (Courtesy of the National Archives at College Park, Record Group 65F, Box 1, Folder 12, #5.)

in a memorandum Tamm wrote for Hoover on April 7, 1939, the day after the shooting. Concerned about the "technical arrest" charges and the proceedings of a coroner's inquest scheduled for April 8, Tamm and Norris together concocted testimony to be given by agents at the inquest. Initially, Norris said he advised his men that the request to appear at the inquest was not a subpoena and told his men not to appear. Tamm told Norris that the agents should testify at the inquest. The problem of only one agent firing at Dickson was a concern, Tamm said. Tamm told Norris:

> Each man should testify that he can not [sic] say as to who fired the fatal shots. I told Mr. Norris to state that several men fired, but

that it was impossible to determine whose shots killed the fugitive. . . . I requested Mr. Norris to be careful to make clear when the inquest is held at 9 o'clock [April 8] that Dickson was recognized by all the agents when he came out of the hamburger stand; that he was called upon to surrender, . . . and was killed when he attempted to draw his pistol after refusing to give himself up.

Bureau officials must have been concerned that local authorities, perhaps angry because they were not notified of Dickson's presence in St. Louis, might consider filing charges if they could determine which one of the agents actually fired his weapon. Tamm told Norris that while it was not his intention to have any of the agents commit perjury, they were not to disclose the name of the agent who fired if questioned under oath at the inquest. Thus, perjury was in fact the result, since the agents knew very well that only one of the four men, Bush, had fired his weapon. Tamm's original plan was for each agent to testify that "in the confusion, he could not tell whether he fired any shots or not." Hoover underlined that passage and scrawled a note on the memo, pointing out the obvious problem with that plan. "This would sound undesirable as certainly an examination of their guns later would show whether any shots had been fired," Hoover wrote. "I see no reason for us to try to placate the local authorities. Our men had a job to do and they did it, and the criminal was killed in the act of pulling a gun. Tell Norris to stand up and not be apologetic to anyone."

Tamm and Norris, it appears, did not share Hoover's confidence about the circumstances of the shooting since they took further steps to assure a coroner's finding that the agent who fired was justified in his actions. Norris enlisted the assistance of St. Louis Assistant US Attorney Herman H. Freer to deal with the issue that only one agent had fired. Norris "was advised by Freer that there is no reason why we should have to testify as to who fired the shots. . . . He thinks it can be arranged whereby the agents will not be required to testify as to these facts," Tamm told Hoover in a memorandum on the morning of the inquest. It was FBI policy to withhold the names of agents who were responsible for the death of accused criminals. That policy, of course, did not extend to testimony under oath. So to avoid identifying Bush as the agent who killed Dickson, Bureau officials arranged for a friendly hearing and agreed that agents would lie and testify that all four agents had fired.

St. Louis newspaper reports the morning after the shooting featured a photograph of Dickson's "arsenal" provided by the FBI, two revolvers and eleven bullets. The *St. Louis Globe-Democrat* on April 7 framed its story in Dillingeresque terms, featuring what they called a "woman in black" who lured Dickson into a trap. Dickson was beaten to the draw by FBI agents, according to the *Globe-Democrat* front-page story. "We killed him or he would have killed us," Norris told reporters. Norris described an "anonymous" phone call that led agents to the shop. Norris was asked specifically about the woman who lured Dickson to the shop. "Gerald B. Norris, chief of the St. Louis office of the FBI, however, denies there was anyone with Dickson," the *Globe-Democrat* reported.

St. Louis Police Department officer Frank Eike was the primary investigator on the Dickson case. His investigation, to put it kindly, was incomplete. Freer questioned Eike, who appeared first at the inquest. "Did you learn any of the particulars relating to the shooting?" Eike responded that his investigation consisted of "just what Norris told me, that four of them fired shots at him when he reached for his gun; they approached him when he came out of the restaurant and told him to put up his hands, they were federal men, and Dickson immediately started reaching for his guns and they shot him." If Eike was recounting Norris's explanation accurately, then Norris lied about the shooting when he claimed that all four agents fired. Eike did ask agents where they found Dickson's two revolvers, a .45 caliber Colt and a .38 caliber snub-nosed Smith & Wesson. "Now did you question any of the agents as to what part of the person of Dickson they found these weapons," Freer asked. "Yes sir; they were on the inside of the waist band of his trousers, the .45 I believe was on the right side and the other one was on the left side of the waist band of his trousers." Asking Norris about the incident was the sum total of Eike's investigation. He did not question witnesses at the scene and neither did his supervisor. No one, not the US attorney or the coroner, asked any follow-up questions.

Next to testify was Cameron, the sole citizen witness called to testify. Concerned about what she might say, Tamm and Norris decided, during their discussions immediately after the shooting, to intimidate her into silence. "I told Mr. Norris that this woman should be brought into the office and given a good scare and that she should be told that she has been quoted in the newspapers as telling some stories that were not true and that if we are going to have to prosecute her for perjury or something, we will do so." Norris further said that "he would be glad to call her to the office as she was a 'little good for nothing' and the reporters had built her up to these statements." To avoid the embarrassment of having to admit that one overzealous agent had unheroically shot an armed public enemy in the back after tracing him to St. Louis by employing a paid informant, the FBI resorted to attempting to intimidate a citizen witness into silence.

To her credit, though, Cameron did not change her story at the inquest. Cameron testified that "the woman in black," Naomi, entered the shop before Dickson, looked around, and left. She walked up and down the street and returned five minutes later. She sat down and Dickson joined her within a couple of minutes. After Dickson paid the check, Cameron testified, Dickson left first and Naomi ran out the door to the FBI agents and said, "That is your man." Cameron continued, "Dickson started to run, it seemed as though he was trying to get away." Cameron said she heard an FBI agent shout "Stick them up" and then saw Dickson turn and run to the right (north) and very soon after she heard two shots. The woman in black then came back into the shop. Cameron noted that the shop was crowded, begging the question (that was never asked) about what other witnesses inside and out on the sidewalk saw. Ultimately, Cameron's testimony was simply ignored by the St. Louis County coroner.

Norris testified after Cameron. Under questioning, Norris claimed that he had received an "anonymous" phone call at 6:45 p.m. informing him that Dickson would be at the shop. Norris said he walked by the window of the shop and was able to see Dickson inside. "I did not think there was any doubt about it as far as facial identification could be made," Norris said. Contrary to what he told Tamm, Norris claimed that he had time to station his agents "opposite the door of the stand" and that he "placed them in a position where pedestrians would not be injured if they would pass by there." In his report to Tamm, Norris said the agents were not yet positioned when Dickson walked out and were standing near the alley just south of the hamburger shop door. Norris again made no mention of Naomi, claiming that Dickson simply emerged from the shop and they ordered him to "Stick them up."

Norris pantomimed what he said Dickson did next. While Cameron told reporters and testified that Dickson turned north and ran, an action that fits the descriptions of his wounds, Norris claimed that Dickson crouched "and swung around as though he were heading into a position to fire at us and kill us and when he did that we fired shots at him and he fell on the sidewalk and we disarmed him and took two guns off of him." Note that Norris's testimony implied that the guns were taken away, as if they were in his hands, an implication inconsistent with what was observed by Officer Eike and by the ambulance crew who reported that the guns were still in Dickson's waistband. Furthermore, Norris's claim that "we" fired shots is simply untrue.

"From the hospital, I went directly to my office in order to report to my superior," Norris said. "I called Mr. Hoover in Washington, D.C., and told him of the occurrence and Mr. Bush and some of the other agents were in attendance at the time and assisted with the preparation and so forth, and later I went to the police station to report to Officer Eike." Norris, of course, did not speak to Hoover but to Tamm. He did confirm with that statement, though, that he conferred with FBI headquarters before speaking at all with St. Louis Police. Asked directly by Freer about the "woman in black," Norris claimed he did not interview her and did not know where she went after the shooting. He denied that the woman in black identified Dickson before the shooting. "No sir, I honestly don't believe that that occurred." Regarding Dickson's character, Norris misleadingly described the Topeka shooting, in which forty-eight shots were fired by police, as a "shooting scrape," implying that Dickson had been the shooter. Norris described Dickson as a "very desperate character." Freer asked if Dickson was violent. "He would take your life if he had the slightest opportunity?" Freer asked. "Yes, sir," Norris responded.

After Norris finished, Bush, Pratt, and Cochran testified, repeating the lie that they knew nothing of a "woman in black" at the scene and testifying that FBI regulations prohibited them from saying whether or not they had fired their guns. Cochran was asked specifically whether he knew how many shots had been fired. "I do not know, not exactly," Cochran said. Through that intermediary and in direct discussions before the inquest, St. Louis Police Department officers were fed false information alleging that Dickson was known to have been a murderer. Officer Arthur L. Abbott was asked what he knew about Dickson before the events of April 6. "Yes, he was known as a desperate bank robber and killer, and we had a number of circulars on him." Dickson was never accused of any gun violence. While he had repeatedly used the threat of violence in the commission of his crimes, Dickson's most violent criminal act was losing his temper and punching a driver's license examiner who taunted him about his criminal record.

With Cameron silenced and local police primed to offer testimony of Dickson's vicious nature, a favorable outcome of the coroner's inquest was a foregone conclusion. "SAC Norris called and advised that the inquest is over and went along very smoothly," Tamm reported in a memorandum to Hoover. "The coroner found that Dickson met his death at the hands of the Agents who were performing their duty and that the shooting was entirely justified. The Coroner's records show that Dickson was resisting arrest and is very complete with respect to his criminal record, character, et cetera." Tamm noted that Norris spoke to the judge, who was "gracious" about not requiring him to disclose which of the agents actually shot Dickson.

Having eliminated any possibility of embarrassment, the FBI was free to tout its success in finding and eliminating a public enemy.

Bureau publicists in the Crime Records Section did just that, issuing a series of radio scripts and press releases and collaborating with magazine, book, and even comic book authors to retell the Bureau's version of the Dickson shooting. As time passed, the story, which had been sanitized by Norris and Tamm immediately following the shooting, evolved as it was retold. In Frederick L. Collins's 1943 book *The FBI in Peace and War*, Dickson merely "went for" his guns before being shot. In the Bureau's official "Interesting Case" memorandum last edited in September 1948, Dickson "endeavored to secure one of his own weapons in an attempt to give further battle to the arresting Agents, but his failing strength was not sufficient for this effort." In a radio "interview" script authored by the Bureau's public relations agents in 1955, Dickson "reached for" his gun "as he had done successfully in the past." In his memoir, *FBI Man: A Personal History*, Special Agent Cochran claimed that Dickson had "vowed he would never be taken alive." When confronted by agents, according to Cochran, Dickson "jerked behind a woman, his hands on his guns. She screamed, and pulled free, and he ran back a step and his guns were pulled out." After the shooting, according to Cochran, "[Dickson] lay on his back, his eyes closed tight, his hands on his weapons, one leg cramped under him, his hat by his side."[3] In fact, Dickson's guns were found by the ambulance crew who loaded up his body. According to their testimony at the inquest, both of Dickson's guns were still tucked in the waistband of his pants under his jacket. In addition to promotional and nonfiction books, the Dickson case eventually became fodder for everything from comic books to restaurant menus. An FBI memorandum issued in 1945 as source material for a *This Is Your FBI* radio show script added an additional and particularly creative fictional detail. According to the author, Ben attempted to use Naomi as a shield between himself and agents, a particularly cowardly detail that was not included in any account of the shooting before that.

James and Darwin Dickson were working at the family farm near Auburn when they learned of Ben's death via a telephone call from a relative. A few minutes later, a reporter called to confirm the shooting.

"You're sure it was Ben they shot?" James Dickson asked the *Topeka Daily Capital* reporter, who wrote that James inquired "anxiously, a trace of hope in his voice." Darwin Dickson told the reporter that the family had not expected to see Ben again. "We knew that he was hunted thruout [*sic*] the country, and we expected that he would be slain." James Dickson told the reporter that they would withhold the news from Ben's mother in fear that the shock would further damage her health. James and Darwin Dickson's comments appeared on the front page of the April 7 *Topeka Daily Capital*. According to Richard Dickson, his grandfather returned to work at Topeka High School the following week and, understanding that students were likely to be curious, tearfully told his students that indeed the slain bank robber had been his son. Back in Jefferson City, prison officials made a note on Ben's ID card that he had been shot by FBI agents. "Deceased," they wrote, then added a flourish and "Finis."

Gloria Cameron was not the only person who saw something less than heroic in the circumstances of Dickson's shooting. On April 8, 1939, John W. Owens, editor of the *Baltimore Sun*, wrote an editorial headlined "Monotonous Tale" criticizing the FBI's frequent and, in Owens's mind, reckless use of force against fugitives:

> Curiously enough, local policemen and detectives rarely find it necessary to shoot and kill desperadoes with whom they frequently deal. . . . In the case of Ben Dickson, the man who they got yesterday, one G-Man at least was with him in the restaurant where he had his last mortal meal. One would think a tap with a blackjack might have been feasible. Or that a revolver leveled at him might have persuaded him that resistance was useless. As we say, we don't pretend to know. But we do know that a killing by G-Men, however quick, cheap, and effective, is not the method provided by law for disposing of criminals.

In another example of the Bureau's sensitivity to any criticism that suggested it used its power recklessly, Hoover's public relations staff responded with a five-page letter to Owens and the *Sun* over Hoover's signature. In the letter, Hoover's Crime Records staff portrayed Dickson as a vicious killer, claiming he had "engaged in a gun battle" with Topeka Police at the Ace tourist camp, despite the fact that Dickson did not return fire when police fired forty-eight shots at him. The letter added a rumor that Dickson planned to blow up the Missouri State Penitentiary. And the letter quoted the account concocted by Norris and Tamm, claiming that Dickson had pulled a .38 caliber automatic pistol on the agents, who fired in self-defense, and comparing Ben to famed outlaw Baby Face Nelson, who murdered two FBI agents when they attempted to capture him.

The Bureau's sensitivity to charges that it recklessly killed criminals is demonstrated by a paragraph in the Dickson Interesting Case Memorandum #7-2561: "Dickson was the sixteenth criminal shot in self-defense by Special Agents of the FBI during a five-year period in which twenty-three thousand criminals were apprehended and convicted by the FBI. Each of the sixteen criminals who met his death in this manner chose to resist arrest rather than to submit to apprehension and was mortally wounded in gun battle with the Special Agents." The juxtaposition of sixteen with twenty-three thousand surely does demonstrate that such incidents were rare, but the circumstances of Dickson's shooting raise questions as to how many of those sixteen were justified.

The most common response by news reporters and editors, though, was to uncritically cheer the Bureau's shooting of Dickson. For example, on April 8, 1939, *Memphis Commercial Appeal* associate editor Jack Carley published an editorial headlined "They Can Expect It." "When the Federal Bureau of Investigation pins the label of public enemy on a man he can expect one of two things, imprisonment or death," Carley wrote in an editorial published April 8, 1939. "[The FBI] has no squeamishness about liquidating known criminals who refuse to submit peacefully. How it succeeds in 'putting the finger' on those it seeks, whether through women in brown, black, red or any other color, is immaterial to the average law-abiding citizen." In almost every case, newspaper reporters and editors nationwide praised the FBI for the shooting and uncritically repeated the Bureau's claims about the "vicious" Ben Dickson.

Newspapers helpfully picked up on details of the shooting and immediately linked Ben to a more famous, and far more villainous, outlaw. According to the April 7 *St. Louis Globe-Democrat*, Ben was "lured into a trap of the federal agents by a 'woman in black' like John Dillinger was caught in a [*sic*] FBI agents' trap in Chicago by a 'woman in red.'"

One of the many odd things about the St. Louis shooting of Ben Dickson was the fact that the four agents on the scene seemed to have forgotten entirely about Dickson's so-called gun moll wife, Stella. "Sure shot Stella" was considered Public Enemy No. 2 by the Bureau, but Norris and his team of agents made no contingency to search for her before or in the aftermath of the shooting until she drove past them at high speed heading north on Euclid Avenue. In fact, she had been parked down the street the entire time they had stood near the alley outside of the Yankee System shop making plans to arrest Ben. It is a very compact area, with narrow streets and short blocks. The Yankee System Hamburger Shop was located at the midpoint of the block, meaning that the Dicksons' car with Stella in it was likely parked less than one hundred feet south of the scene of the shooting. Once Ben had been identified, a glance down the street would have quickly revealed "sure shot Stella," the so-called gun moll, waiting in a car less than one-half block away. It also seems odd that four trained FBI special agents did not notice when, immediately after the shooting, Stella started the car and turned the south-facing car around to head north, surely not an easy or quick task with a large car on a narrow street. Instead, they thought of Stella only as she drove by on Euclid Avenue, only slightly more than the width of a parked car away from where the agents stood near Ben's body.

Although they got a late start, the Bureau moved quickly in the hours after Ben's killing to locate Stella. Within a few hours of Ben's death, a wiretap was placed on the Redenbaugh telephone and both the Redenbaugh and Dickson homes were placed under twenty-four-hour surveillance. Agents reinterviewed James Dickson, Ben's brother

Darwin, and the Redenbaughs. Several of Stella's school friends from eighth grade, Roma Richards, Peggy Kane, and Helen Stobbe, were questioned. With the acquiescence of Topeka Post Office officials, the FBI once again intercepted and read mail destined for the Redenbaugh and Dickson homes.

7

HOME TO MOTHER

Stella drove away from her husband's shooting feeling distraught and desperate to get home to her mother. Without her much older husband with whom she played the role of a relatively mature and sophisticated bride, Stella reverted to the timid and sometimes petulant teenager she had been before her marriage. In Topeka, Hattie Redenbaugh learned of Ben's death via a radio report. On April 7, Redenbaugh told the *Topeka Daily Capital* that she still could not believe her daughter was a fugitive sought by J. Edgar Hoover's FBI. "She's so young, only six-teen," she said. "She'd never been in trouble before. I think she was afraid to get in touch with me after [the tourist camp incident before] Thanksgiving for fear I would turn against her." Hattie expressed re-gret at Ben's death. "I couldn't have asked for a better son-in-law," Redenbaugh said. "He was courteous and intelligent, and seemed very much in love with Estelle. He always was thoughtful; I was terribly shocked to learn that he had a police record and was sought."

After she sped away from the scene of her husband's death, Stella drove around until she found a garage for rent at 5615 Cates Avenue, about two miles from the hamburger shop. She paid the owner three dollars and spent the night in her car parked in the garage. The next morning, Stella walked to a nearby busy street, hailed a cab, and went to the St. Louis Airport hoping to catch a flight to Kansas City. "I saw a policeman there so immediately left in the same cab and drove around a while and had the taxi driver take me to a travel bureau where I finally made an arrangement with some people for a ride to Kansas City." The taxi dropped Stella at the Mike Longo Travel Bureau, where she hired Hoffman to drive her to Kansas City. Even as the 110-pound, 16-year-old widow was making her emotional journey toward home, the FBI continued to maintain that Stella was a violent and dangerous fugitive. Norris, whose bungling had allowed her to escape after the botched attempt to arrest Dickson, told reporters that Stella was "just as tough a customer as Ben was. Estelle Dickson is wanted just as badly as her husband was." On April 9, after her capture, the *Kansas City Star* reported that "peace officers in several states have been talking of Estelle Dickson as the most feared 'gun girl' since Bonnie Parker."

Unarmed, Stella was arrested by FBI agents as she waited in Hoffman's car in downtown Kansas City on April 7. Easter shoppers crowding the downtown sidewalks were no doubt unaware that the FBI's Public Enemy No. 2 had been captured in their midst. "I knew the minute he stopped he was going to get a federal man to arrest me," Stella told FBI agents. "I didn't care. I just sat in the car. I knew if I got out and tried to get to Topeka myself, I wouldn't get there alive and I wanted to see my mother." In the April 9 *Topeka Daily Capital*, Hattie Redenbaugh said she was not surprised that her daughter was taken into custody without incident, FBI claims that she was "extremely dangerous" notwithstanding. "I knew Estelle would be taken, and I knew exactly the way she would act," Redenbaugh told reporters. "By that I mean that I knew they would find Estelle unarmed and that she would offer no resistance to those who arrested her." Stella carried seventy dollars in cash and wore three rings when she was arrested. Her wedding ring was set with seven diamonds. She was wearing a gold Bulova wristwatch with four diamonds and had a pin in the shape of "Estelle" on her dress.

She also carried the key to the couple's home in New Orleans at 615 Exposition Boulevard. Lastly, Stella carried a copy of an amateurish but poignant poem written by her late husband titled "In These Eyes."

In the Eyes of Men I am not just, and I should not live
But in your eyes O life I see justification
You have taught me that my path is right if I am true to you.

FBI agents, spurred on by Department of Justice attorneys who feared the sixteen-year-old would invoke coverture as her defense, moved quickly to take a statement. Based on a principle from English common law, coverture was sometimes used as a defense in criminal cases to assert that a wife had been coerced by her husband into committing a crime and thus was exempt from punishment. At the very least, coverture offered the potential as an exculpatory argument to minimize Stella's sentence if she pleaded guilty. In a letter written the day before Stella's capture, US Attorney George Philip urged the FBI to quickly get a statement from Stella before she could assert coverture. "We hope that the Bureau of Investigation men can be instructed to get information from Mrs. Dickson as soon as she is apprehended that she was a willing participant in the robbery at Elkton, South Dakota, and Brookings, South Dakota," Philip wrote to Werner Hanni, SAC of the Bureau's Aberdeen, South Dakota, field office. "The reason this should be procured is that our District Judge instructs very strongly on the coverture rule." The last sentence was underlined by FBI Director J. Edgar Hoover, who received a copy of the letter from Hanni a few days later.

Federal Bureau of Investigation agents, thus hurried along by prosecutors, questioned Stella immediately after she was examined by a physician, without an attorney present, and before her mother arrived in Kansas City. Alone and without legal or parental guidance, Stella agreed to furnish a confession that has been frequently quoted in this narrative. In her sixteen-page statement, Stella acknowledged her part in the two bank robberies and the kidnapping of three men in Michigan. She denied any knowledge of stolen cars and said all of the couple's crimes were initiated by her husband. After she had completed writing her confession, Hattie and Lester Redenbaugh, Stella's brother, Junior, and the family attorney arrived in Kansas City. The Redenbaugh entourage met Stella at the Jackson County Jail and, in the presence of FBI Special Agent L. B. Reed, who insisted on being present, talked to her for two hours. According to Reed's report on the meeting Hattie was angry that her daughter had been questioned and had issued a written statement without parents present or the benefit of legal advice. "Mrs. Redenbaugh then asked the writer many questions in the presence of her daughter concerning what sentence might be given Stella upon conviction of bank robbery or kidnapping," Reed wrote.

Stella volunteered that she had mailed some of the couple's remaining money to herself in care of general delivery at Lawrence, Kansas, a short drive from Topeka. "You have been so nice to me," she allegedly told Reed, "I'll tell you where some of the money is." She did not remember how much money was in the package. Ben had urged her to mail herself the money, Stella said, so that she would not be arrested with money in her possession. The package, containing $850, was picked up by FBI agents and turned over to the US attorney in South Dakota. On April 10, 1939, Stella appeared before a federal commissioner. Reporters were allowed to follow her up to the commissioner's office door and to observe while she and her parents discussed the situation with authorities. Stella was advised by the commissioner and her attorneys to waive extradition to South Dakota, where she would face bank robbery charges in federal district court in Sioux Falls, the state's largest city, located about fifty miles south of Brookings. The US Commissioner at Kansas City set Stella's bond at $25,000 returnable at Sioux Falls.

Some April 11 newspaper accounts published alongside photos of Stella at the commissioner's office noted the contrast between the wispy, quiet, childlike Stella Mae Dickson they saw and the violent gun moll the FBI had so frequently described. Where newspapers had previously published FBI assertions that Stella was dangerous and ruthless, reporters and photographers in Kansas City saw for themselves that she was in fact a thin, sickly looking sixteen-year-old. Throughout the meeting with the commissioner, Stella sat in her mother's lap like a child. A series of *Kansas City Star* photos showed Stella with her mother at the courthouse. In a photo on the front page of the April 11 *Topeka Daily Capital*, Hattie Redenbaugh appeared to be crying and Stella appeared, as one might expect of a sixteen-year-old widow accused of serious felonies, shell-shocked and bewildered. In another, Stella, looking tiny in comparison to the FBI agents accompanying her, is steered into the commissioner's office by Reed and another agent. Yet another photo shows Stella looking directly into the camera, wide-eyed, as her mother, appearing stricken, sits next to her and a stern-looking Lester Redenbaugh stands in the background. A *Topeka Daily Capital* reporter who overheard the meeting reported in the April 11 story that when the commissioner read the charges and the agreement to waive extradition, Stella asked, "What does that mean?" and after being told it meant she would be returned to South Dakota, she said in a quiet voice, "I'm willing to do that." Stella signed the documents, the reporter noted, with careful penmanship.

In addition to Stella's youthful appearance, reporters made note of her clothing, which was faded and rumpled, and of her hair, which was dyed brown with blonde roots. According to the *Daily Capital*, as she removed her dirty, gray-and-white lumber jacket, Stella tried to hold her dress together with one hand. The buttons, which could be made into weapons, had been removed by jailers. "They took my buttons off at the county jail," she said and explained that the dress had gotten dirty while she slept in the car on her way to Kansas City. Her shabby dress was a stark contrast to the glamorous image built up by FBI and newspaper reports. As reported in the April 11 *Topeka Daily Capital*, in response to a question from the US Commissioner, Stella said her height as "almost 5-feet, 3-inches tall, but I'll grow a little more." Throughout the courthouse meeting, Stella could be seen attempting to console her mother even as Hattie tried to avoid the cameras. Stella's aunt Ethel Irwin, who served as the family's spokesperson with the press, told reporters that afternoon that "her family was deeply shocked at her marriage to Dickson. She was married at an impressionable age." According to the April 11 *Kansas City Star*, Hattie Redenbaugh reportedly said, "Now she can straighten out after a bad start, poor kid."

Perhaps attempting to highlight their daughter's youth, the Redenbaughs allowed reporters to meet with her later that day. Stella told the reporters she had waited in the car for her husband to return from his meeting with Naomi. "As Johnny had been gone for some time, I got anxious," she told FBI agents. "I turned the car around to start back towards the hamburger stand. I heard some shots and as I drove by the hamburger stand I saw Johnny on the ground." In that April 10 interview, Stella became emotional when she told the story. "It seems like I looked at him a year lying there on the sidewalk," she said. "I can remember everything about him—the way he looked." Stella told reporters she was angry at the "woman in black" who had betrayed Ben. "I hope the reward money she may get will justify her feeling for having a man's life taken," she said.[1]

Although just sixteen, Stella faced the possibility of the death penalty for kidnapping and life in prison for each count of bank robbery. In an April 11, 1939, letter, US Attorney George Philip of Rapid City, South Dakota, reminded the FBI that the federal judge who would hear Stella's case was an exponent of the coverture defense. Stella's initial confession, rushed by FBI agents, asserted that she was a willing participant in the crimes. After a discussion with her attorney, Stella issued a second statement with few factual changes but with a tone more befitting a coverture defense. "Johnny planned each of these bank robberies and I was with him during each robbery only because he told me to go with him," Stella wrote on April 13, 1939. "I did not plan to go into either of those banks but did go into each of them because Johnny stayed in each bank so long I got worried about him and went into the banks to look for him." She added that she would never have entered a bank to rob it on her own. While it is undoubtedly true that she would not have hatched a bank robbery scheme on her own, Stella did voluntarily (and apparently as part of Ben's plan) enter the Brookings bank during the robbery.

Stella did add several details in particular that did not show up in her previous confession, stating, "[Johnny] frequently got mad at me and said if I left him he would kill me and said he would kill anybody who helped me leave him." She said that two Lake Benton men, "Farmer Reid" and "Wally," had been present when Ben made that statement and could testify to that fact. Stella said several times she had asked Ben for money so she could visit her mother in Topeka and added that Ben hid the car keys from her so she could not sneak away. According to Stella, her friend Mary Robinson from Stockton, California, could testify to that fact. She also said she had never fired a pistol in her life, asserting that the Lake Benton photo of her holding a rifle in one hand and a pistol in the other was posed. "The only pistol I ever handled belonged to Johnny," she said. She added more emphasis to another detail from her initial confession, stating that to her knowledge, Ben had never given her a significant share of the robbery proceeds, only providing her with spending money and advising her to mail the $850 to herself if he was captured or killed.

FBI officials, of course, were skeptical of the new confession. "Through her attorneys, Stella Mae sought to avoid punishment relying upon two defenses," Bureau publicists wrote in a press release after the case was settled. "One, that she was of such an age as to be considered a juvenile under the terms of the federal Juvenile Delinquency statute and the other that she was entitled to protection of the ancient coverture rule which implies a wife is acting upon the compulsion of her husband if she participates in a crime with him." In fact the two confessions complemented each other in that the first demonstrated her loyalty to her much older husband and the second plausibly explained her participation in the crimes she was accused of as having been coerced by Ben. That she was a minor when the crimes were committed was simply a fact.

Initially, US Attorney George Philip argued that coverture did not apply in the case of Stella Mae Dickson. In addition to legal arguments based on contemporary cases, Philip concocted a unique argument based on a convenient invocation of women's rights:

If the protection of coverture ever did apply to a wife on trial
in the federal courts, it has no application now, in view of the
changed status of women. It may be that a husband can cajole his
wife to her detriment. No one but a bachelor judge would even
indulge, in this day and age, the legal fiction that a husband can so
dominate his wife as to compel her to commit, or to participate in
a heinous felony.

That novel and unsupported argument aside, the question of whether
a coverture defense applied in Stella's case was significant enough that
on May 27, 1939, Philip wrote to Attorney General Frank Murphy for
guidance. Philip told Murphy, "We are in serious difficulty to determine a policy in this case." Philip said negotiations with the judge and
with the defense counsel had not resulted in any agreement on how the
case should proceed. Philip said he did have some sympathy for Stella.
He wrote, essentially making the argument for a coverture defense:

I think we may safely assume that at her years, she would never
have engaged in bank robbery or any other crimes of armed violence, but for the fact that, at the age of fifteen, she was misled
into marrying an outlaw like Ben Dickson, who was twenty-seven
years of age at the time of his death, and who was the son of a high
school professor at Topeka, not known to the girl or her family to
be engaged in crime.

Oddly, Philip said that he and the judge agreed that because Stella lived
in Kansas, it would "be difficult for this Court to keep adequate track
of her" if she were sentenced to probation. But Philip was not set on
a prison sentence, either. "Perhaps, regardless of the enormity of the
crimes charged against her, she should be treated as the person that she
is," he wrote, suggesting that the "person that she is" was just a child.
"I am puzzled and am looking to the Department for light." Murphy's
deputy, Welly K. Hopkins, wrote back on Murphy's behalf on June 3,
1939, noting that the Board of Parole in Kansas could easily monitor
Stella's probation, eliminating that argument in favor of a prison sentence but otherwise refusing to make any sentencing recommendation.
It is likely that the reluctance of the attorney general and his staff to

make a recommendation to Philip was related to the obstinance of a man Murphy ostensibly supervised but who, in reality, held much more power than the attorney general, FBI Director Hoover.

Hoover's long-advocated positions urging maximum penalties for juvenile offenders and opposing parole and probation were well known. In addition, he sent Murphy a memorandum, citing the expense of the FBI's lengthy investigation and "requesting that this case be vigorously prosecuted and all the facts concerning the types of crimes committed by Stella Mae Dickson be brought to the attention of the court at the time she is sentenced." Clearly, Hoover would not stand for a sentence of probation, no matter the circumstances. The day after Murphy received Hoover's memorandum urging "vigorous" prosecution, another of the attorney general's deputies, O. John Rogge, wrote to Philip asserting that whether or not Stella was responsible for the robberies, she had also been involved in the kidnappings in Michigan. Rogge, without addressing whether coverture would apply in that case, urged that Stella be sentenced to a minimum of ten years in prison. In what was perhaps a purposeful oversight, Rogge's letter did not arrive until after Stella's sentencing, thus affording the attorney general the political cover of having urged a harsh sentence as cover in his relationship with Hoover no matter what the judge and prosecutor determined.

One week after her capture at Kansas City, Stella had been moved to South Dakota. Her imminent arrival in Sioux Falls created significant public interest. Newspaper stories announced that she would arrive on a train within days. Crowds gathered daily at the Milwaukee Railroad Depot in downtown Sioux Falls, awaiting a glimpse of Stella. South Dakota officials feared an incident if Stella were brought to Sioux Falls and instead diverted her to a newly constructed jail in Mitchell, seventy miles west of Sioux Falls. On May 19, the *Sioux Falls Daily Argus Leader* described Stella's arrival in Mitchell: "Stella Mae looked more like a school girl than a gun moll waiting the proceedings of the court. . . . She is a small girl, short and not very heavy and wore a small black hat set back on her blonde hair, which made her appear no older than the 16 years she claims."

On April 20, Brookings bank officials Dorothy Coffey and John

Torsey, along with the three Elkton girls who saw Stella outside the Corn Exchange Bank, arrived in Mitchell and all identified her as the woman involved in the robberies. "It was learned that the FBI agents dressed Estelle in the clothes found in the abandoned automobile [from St. Joseph] in order to help witnesses identify her," the *Brookings Daily Register* reported that day. "The clothing was said to be the same she wore during the robberies."

During the ensuing months of legal give-and-take, Stella's attorneys protested her innocence and argued for leniency under the coverture rule. In May, she was transported to Sioux Falls, where her attorney, Chet Morgan of Mitchell, discussed the case with US Attorney Philip. In another story, *Argus Leader* reporters noted on August 21 that federal officials (likely referring to Philip) "were surprised by Stella's youthful appearance and the cheapness of her wearing apparel. Both of which, in the light of her record and reputed hauls made in the couple's alleged bank robbing forays, seemed singularly inconsistent. Striking too, was the childlike attitude and actions of the girl, whose demeanor as she walked in the marshal's office was like that of a youngster detained after school for a minor infraction."

Under pressure from Hoover and the Justice Department, and even as Philip expressed his own doubts about whether to support a harsh sentence, US District Judge Lee A. Wyman urged prosecutors and the defense to redouble their efforts to reach an agreement. On August 21, 1939, Stella Mae Dickson appeared in federal district court in Deadwood, South Dakota, more than four hundred miles west of Brookings, and pled guilty to two counts of bank robbery. Wyman, citing Stella's youth and the corrupting influence of her husband and claiming it was a lenient judgment, sentenced her to two ten-year sentences in prison to be served concurrently.

While Rogge's letter had not reached Philip until after the sentencing, FBI files show that the Department of Justice had sent its recommendation for a prison sentence to Wyman via telegram before the sentencing. The judge, Philip later reported in a letter to Murphy, "took the position that the Department [of Justice] had expressed itself as to the proper form of punishment by designating the institution in which the defendant should be imprisoned." Finally, Murphy's deputy Rogge, clearly playing both sides of the issue, wrote Philip on August 25 asserting that the harsh sentence (that he had recommended in the late-arriving letter and in the telegram to the judge) was an error and that a jury should have determined Stella's punishment.

In the end, Hoover's presence loomed over the proceedings as Murphy and his deputies maneuvered around their US attorney in South Dakota, who had expressed support for a coverture-influenced, lenient sentence of probation. Even as they claimed in letters to Philip to oppose prison for Stella, Murphy's deputies intervened by directly influencing Judge Wyman via telegram to impose a harsh sentence on sixteen-year-old Stella. Murphy thus saved himself from suffering Hoover's wrath without having to rebuke his US attorney. Cowed by the power of the FBI director, Murphy was able to take credit for the harsh sentence with Hoover while denying responsibility to Philip. Stella's attorney, meanwhile, had no inkling of the internecine battle taking place between Hoover and Murphy or of the attorney general's intervention with the judge. Obviously, any communication between the attorney general and the judge without the defense attorney's knowledge would be inappropriate at best and at worst would raise serious ethical concerns. Meanwhile, oblivious to the political maneuvering that transformed her sentence from probation to prison, then-seventeen-year-old widow Stella Mae Dickson arrived at the US Women's Reformatory at Alderson, West Virginia, six days later to begin serving her sentence.

Hoover, though, was not through trying to influence her prosecution. Notified that a guilty plea was imminent in the bank robbery cases, Hoover wrote to Assistant Attorney General Rogge and urged that the sixteen-year-old also be prosecuted for kidnapping.

> This Bureau conducted a very exhaustive investigation entailing a considerable expense and loss of Agents' time during the seven-month period that Benjamin James [*sic*] Dickson was sought,

and during which time he was sheltered and aided by Stella Mae Dickson. I am requesting that [the kidnapping] case be vigorously prosecuted and all of the facts concerning the types of crimes committed by Stella Mae Dickson be brought to the attention of the Court.

The Michigan US attorney ultimately decided not to prosecute Stella for the kidnappings, which were clearly orchestrated by her husband.

Before Stella's legal case began to wind its way through the courts, Ben Dickson was buried in Auburn, Kansas. A gusty wind chilled his family and friends at his burial on April 11, 1939. Dickson, twenty-seven, who had been described by his widow as a "philosopher and idealist," was buried alongside his grandparents and great-grandparents in the family plot at Auburn Cemetery, about one-half mile west of the town of Auburn on Southwest Hodges Street. The cemetery is set in a beautiful spot, quiet, tree-lined, and peaceful, on a high point on the rolling hills of northeast Kansas. Grave markers in the cemetery face the setting sun with an expansive view of the rolling farmland to the west. Those present at the burial included Dickson's grieving family, with the exception of Ben's ailing mother, who wasn't told of his death, and his widow, whose request to attend was denied by the FBI. Instead, Stella sat in a cell at the Jackson County Jail in Kansas City awaiting extradition to South Dakota. Stella's parents attended the burial along with several friends of the family. The funeral earlier that day at the Wall-Diffenderfer Mortuary chapel was attended, according to the April 11 *Topeka Daily Capital*, by an overflow crowd estimated at more than six hundred and included most of the faculty of Topeka High School, there to support their colleague James Dickson. Many of Stella's school friends attended the funeral. One of Stella's friends, the newspaper reported, most likely Elizabeth Musick, sobbed uncontrollably at the back of the chapel. The newspaper reported that Ben's casket was "buried in flowers." "To many there it was not a notorious gunman, it was not Public Enemy No. 1 whom they mourned, but rather the carefree, tousle-headed son of respected parents, the

Ben Dickson's grave at Auburn Cemetery west of Auburn, Kansas. (Photo by the author.)

boy who got off on the wrong foot and couldn't seem to get back in step," the *Daily Capital* editorialized. "Thou art a God who understands heartaches and shadows," Rev. William E. Dull told mourners. "Thy love and thy mercy excels. We pray for this family that their troubled hearts may have the balm of the Physician of Nazareth." As the mourners wandered back to their cars, the newspaper reported, workmen shouldered their shovels to finish the burial.

After four months in jail in Missouri and South Dakota, Stella arrived at the Alderson, West Virginia, Federal Industrial Institution for Women on August 28, 1939, marking her seventeenth birthday on the train en route. Located about thirty miles northwest of Blacksburg in southeastern West Virginia, the Federal Industrial Institution for Women at Alderson, now called Federal Prison Camp–Alderson, is nestled up against the Greenbrier River in a hilly, forested, and picturesque setting. The institution occupies five hundred acres, two hundred of which were given to the government by the citizens of Alderson. What is now a minimum-security prison opened in 1927 as a women's reformatory, part of the reformatory movement in which inmates took classes and practiced trades during their incarceration with a goal of rehabilitation and early release.

Alderson addressed a severe shortage of federal prison space for women in the 1930s. Before the opening of the Alderson reformatory, women prisoners were often housed in men's federal prisons, a situation that created difficult security concerns, exposing female inmates to significant danger of sexual exploitation and physical injury. The Alderson Federal Industrial Institution for Women featured dormitory-style accommodations for prisoners, was modeled after boarding schools, and featured a curriculum of vocational training classes. Classes offered included sewing, laundry, cooking, table service, household economics, stenography and typewriting, nurse's training, metalworking, painting, and general farmwork. Academic instruction was limited to English and math. Prisoners were housed on the unfenced grounds in brick cottages that resemble college dormitories of the era. The layout of the buildings also resembles a small college with two green spaces crisscrossed by sidewalks and ringed by the prison "cottages" and other buildings. Inside each thirty-room cottage, women were provided with a private room including a single bed, small desk, and dresser. Government public relations photographs from the 1940s show Alderson's small general store and tidy dorm rooms complete with curtains and matching radiator covers. In the photos, inmates wear simple dresses and sensible shoes and are shown sewing or reading in their rooms. Alderson's most famous prisoners included jazz singer Billie Holiday, who was incarcerated there on a drug charge in 1947 and 1948, along with World War II propagandists Tokyo Rose and Axis Sally. Later, attempted presidential assassin Lynette "Squeaky" Fromme famously escaped from Alderson, and television personality Martha Stewart served five months in Alderson in 2005 for obstruction of justice. During the 1930s, several other women associated with famed outlaws, including

Federal Reformatory for Women, Alderson, West Virginia. Stella Mae
Dickson spent most of her seven years in prison at Alderson. (Courtesy of
the Library of Congress, Call Number HABS WVA, 45-ALD.V,1-C-1.)

Kathryn Kelly, wife of George "Machine Gun" Kelly, and Bonnie
Parker's sister Billie Jean Parker were housed at Alderson. The authors
of the 1929 *Handbook of American Prisons and Reformatories* judged the
Alderson reformatory as a state-of-the-art institution: "[The facility] is
well adapted to the requirements of a great regenerative enterprise. Its
program is based on humane motives functioning through a thorough
and scientific study of the prisoners. There appears no disposition,
moreover, to forget that the offender is an individual."

Despite the trappings of a boarding school, Alderson was a prison and
inmates' time was scheduled for them, including both traditional school
classes and industrial training. In an admission summary, the warden
summarized Stella's case and concluded that "Subject is a pathetic child

who defies anyone to be sorry for her." Her prison counselors did take Stella's difficult childhood into account as they planned her treatment and activities. Stella's experience in Topeka, a brutal rape followed by dehumanizing treatment for venereal disease and ultimately by public shame, was recounted in her Bureau of Prisons file. In addition, counselors discussed Ben's shooting in St. Louis with Stella. "[Stella] feels that his death by gun fire during the arrest was a brutal attack on the part of the officers," a prison counselor wrote on Stella's first progress report. "It is difficult for her to admit error, and her natural reserve has turned to defiance and assumed indifference." As part of the admission process, Stella was examined by a psychologist. Her IQ was found to be 121 and the psychologist reported that she had a "keen mind." Under a section headed "impressions," though, the psychologist noted that the tumult of events Stella had experienced during the prior three years had forced her to build up impenetrable psychological defenses against the outside world. "The subject through her reticence, abruptness and pert pose, hopes to build around her a hard outside covering. Her natural characteristics show enthusiasm and vivacity along with cleverness and the responsiveness of youth. She will need the guidance of good leaders to teach her self control, obedience and other desirable characteristics."

Stella's first quarterly progress report, filed three months later, on December 29, 1939, showed that she had not let down her defenses. The report indicated that Stella was eligible for parole in December 1942. Her attitude, however, was not good. "[Stella] possesses a blocked personality, thinks everyone is her enemy, and cannot forget the glamour and excitement she experienced while traveling over the country with her young bandit husband until he was killed," a counselor wrote about midway through her time in Alderson. "She is pathetic and tragic." Stella's English teacher reported that she had a tendency to "just sit" or to sketch rather than listen and learn. "There is good rapport among the class members which Stella has tried to spoil," English teacher Miss Smith reported. Her overall attitude was described as "blasé, trying and yet pitiful." Typing and shorthand teacher Miss Ruppenthal noted that Stella was "intelligent but not especially ambitious." And music teacher Miss Linkhous wrote that Stella's "output was practically nothing" and that she had an "insolent, stubborn attitude."

After one year at Alderson, Stella was transferred to the Federal Reformatory for Women at Seagoville, Texas. The Seagoville facility opened in October 1940. While it offered similar courses for its inmates and housed them in dormitories, the physical location of the Seagoville institution was very different from the college campus atmosphere and rolling hills around Alderson. Seagoville is located southeast of Dallas on the stark, flat Texas plain. The weather, of course, was different as well, a significant consideration in the days before air conditioning. While Alderson can be warm in the summer, with temperatures averaging in the low 80s for several weeks, Seagoville averages temperatures of at least 82 degrees from May to October with 90-plus-degree temperatures in June, July, and August. Overall, the Seagoville facility lacked the campus feel of the Alderson reformatory, more closely resembling a traditional prison or military facility.

The counselors at Seagoville, like those in Alderson, seemed unable to understand Stella's lingering anger. Shortly after her arrival, Stella was placed in solitary confinement because she showed an "antagonistic and disrespectful" attitude to a corrections officer. Despite their knowledge of her abuse as a child, her rape by a stranger, and the loss of her husband, counselors seemed unable to comprehend the source of Stella's anger. "She enters into any interview apparently with a preconceived conviction that she is going to be maneuvered out of something, and she consistently misinterprets conversations with officers to support her own beliefs," a counselor wrote in late 1940. Another report began, "Since this inmate's last appearance at classification, she has been placed in seclusion for a period of 64 days." During that time, Stella was given reading materials and spoke briefly to guards but was otherwise alone in the "quarantine" area of the prison. At one point she was given a copy of *The Story of Mankind*, a history of Western civilization written for children by Hendrik van Loon. "It was noticed that many of her comments [on the book] were cynical observations on how little man had learned," her counselor reported. As might be expected, Stella lost considerable weight during her time in solitary, dropping to under 100 pounds from the 122 she weighed when she arrived at Seagoville. Throughout the remainder of her imprisonment, she struggled to keep her weight in a healthy range. Counselors at Seagoville noted that Stella, once she was released from solitary confinement, had only one friend in her dormitory, Elsie Byrom. Their response was to separate the two of them.

On February 19, 1942, President Franklin Delano Roosevelt, in an act that has been judged as a significant blemish on his record, signed Executive Order 9066, which authorized the creation of military exclusion areas. The order was the legal justification for the internment during World War II of noncombatants, primarily Japanese Americans, who refused to leave the West Coast of the United States. Those noncombatants were presumed to be disloyal, forcibly removed from their homes, and placed in internment camps, essentially, and in some cases literally, a prison. In early 1942, the Seagoville reformatory was designated to receive some of those interned American citizens and the reformatory's female inmates were transferred out. In March 1942, Stella was returned to Alderson and served the remainder of her sentence there.

Back at Alderson, counselors reported marked improvement in Stella's attitude by mid-1943. Still, she carried the emotional scars of the multiple traumas of the prior several years. "[Stella] has personality difficulties wherein she assumes an air of indifference and arrogance, but underneath her austerity she is gentle, timid and thirsty for affection and attention," according to a June 17, 1943, progress report. "She wants to be friendly and useful, but in her timid and introversive way does not know how to make the first advance." Stella seemed to enjoy solitary work and was praised for the quality and speed of her work as a bookbinder. "She cherishes being asked to do meticulous things and basks in the attention and praise accorded her when she has done really fine work," the bindery supervisor reported. Sheet metal class was a particular favorite for Stella. "She likes this [sheet metal] class very much and stated she had gained eight pounds since being assigned," her counselor wrote.

One change that appears to have helped Stella adjust and mature was her relationship with a member of the Alderson citizen's advisory board, former Florida Congresswoman Ruth Bryan Owen Rohde. Rohde was the daughter of famed orator and three-time Democratic presidential nominee William Jennings Bryan. She was the first woman elected to Congress from the South and served two terms in the House of Representatives, losing her bid for reelection in 1932 because of her support for the repeal of Prohibition. Before her service in Congress, she served as a war nurse in World War I, was a pioneering filmmaker, and served as an administrator at the University of Miami. After serving in Congress, she was appointed as the US ambassador to Denmark by President Franklin Delano Roosevelt and lived in Denmark for three years, marrying a Dane, Borge Rohde. They moved to West Virginia and lived in a mansion known as The Cedars that was owned by the Rohde family. From 1938 to 1954, Ruth Bryan Owen Rohde served on the Alderson Advisory Board, through which she came to know Stella. For years until her death in 1954, Rohde supplemented Stella's income by hiring her as a seamstress. Among the items Stella left to her longtime neighbor in Kansas City was a signed photograph from Rohde: "To Stella Mae with every good wish from her friend."

A 1945 progress report noted that while Stella had matured, she could still "be so contrary she would try the patience of a saint." As her early release date neared in 1946, Stella, then twenty-four, was considered a model prisoner, "known for her charming personal appearance and her skill at wood and metal work." It was reported that she was loyal to her friends and was willing to defend them when they were threatened and that the other inmates "stand in awe of her." Still, Stella was a loner, choosing to avoid group activities in favor of reading or playing records during her free time. One of her teachers wrote that Stella was "doing very well, but very peculiar in that she can never be engaged in conversation, about work or otherwise, although she is polite at all times, does her work well and seems interested." That pattern

Ruth Bryan Owen Rohde was the daughter of famed orator and presidential candidate William Jennings Bryan. She was the first congresswoman from the South, serving two terms representing her district in Florida. Later, she served on the advisory board of the Federal Reformatory for Women. Rohde took an interest in Stella, hiring her as a seamstress and maintaining contact with her after she left prison. (Courtesy of the Library of Congress, Call Number LC-H25-142275-DA.)

of avoidance of emotional attachments would recur frequently during the remaining decades of Stella's life, concluding with a thirty-three-year stretch during which time she was effectively a recluse, leaving her home only to go to work and attend to other business. On May 2, 1946, twenty-four-year-old Stella was released from prison on parole and finally made her way home to her mother in Topeka. She was discharged from parole in August 1949.

Stella's post-prison life included at least one failed marriage, a long string of hourly jobs, and a continued connection to family in Topeka.[2] After living with her mother and stepfather for almost two years, Stella married a man twenty years her senior and lived with him in Sioux City, Iowa, and then Omaha for several years. Ralph H. Dougherty was a traveling salesman and the two were married on August 1, 1948. Stella later told a neighbor that Dougherty abused her and was irrationally jealous of his attractive and much younger wife. "I left that son-of-a-bitch in a heartbeat," Stella told the neighbor.[3] Stella divorced Dougherty on August 31, 1952. From 1954 to 1962, according to FBI files, she "lived with a married man for about two days each week and frequently went with him on trips." After that, according to her family, Stella avoided men. "She hated men. She had no need for them," Stella's great-niece Gloria Seematter said. Gloria's sister Renee Araiza, who was close to her aunt for many years, said, "She loved us [her nieces] a lot."

Between 1951 and 1962, Stella lived in Omaha, Denver, and three different locations in Kansas City. In 1958, she moved to Kansas City for good. There, Stella worked as a dressmaker. She lived in a modest ranch home she had purchased for $13,995 at 4905 East 40th Terrace in Kansas City. According to city directory listings, Stella had a roommate, Jeannine A. Gray, who worked at the US Marine Corps Recruiting Station in Kansas City.

On May 7, 1962, Stella paid $15,899 to purchase a home at 7338 Sycamore Avenue, right outside the boundary of Raytown, an incorporated city within the footprint of Kansas City. Originally a Santa Fe Trail stop, Raytown is located south of Independence. The town got

Stella Mae Irwin, portrait taken in the late 1940s or early 1950s. Note the
scar on her right forehead at the hairline that she received when struck by a
bullet fragment when she and her husband were fleeing police in Michigan.
(Photo courtesy of Gloria Seematter, from the Araiza family collection.)

its name from William Ray's blacksmith shop, a landmark located at the corner of what is now 63rd Street and Raytown Road. The town was not incorporated as a self-governed community within the Kansas City area until 1950. By the 1960s, when Stella moved to the bordering neighborhood, Raytown covered about ten square miles and had three thousand residents. By 1975, the population of the area had grown to thirty-three thousand. Sycamore Avenue runs north and south and is located between Swope Memorial Golf Course and the Floral Hills Cemetery. After moving to the adjacent neighborhood, Stella worked as a clerk in various Raytown stores for more than thirty years.

About ten blocks long, Sycamore Avenue features a neat row of modest ranch homes, most of them built in the 1950s and 1960s. Stella's 1,100-square-foot home was built in 1954. Located at the northwest corner of East Seventy-Fourth Street and Sycamore Avenue, Stella's house featured a two-car garage, like most of the homes in the neighborhood, and because it was built on a slope, there was a garden-level basement. A chain link fence surrounded the backyard, with another, smaller chain link enclosure nearer the house for her dogs. She made significant improvements to her home, using many of the skills she had learned in prison. According to her family, Stella was skilled at home repair. She fixed the furnace, rebuilt the back deck, installed new cabinets, planted trees and flowers, and generally spruced up the home. "She never hired people to come in and do anything," Renee Araiza said. "If something happened, she would fix it herself." Stella kept a toolbox in her car for emergencies.

For Seematter and her siblings, most of their contact with their great-aunt came in the Redenbaugh home at 2401 Clay Street in Topeka. Richard Araiza, father of Gloria Seematter, Renee Araiza, and one other daughter, is the son of Virginia (Baldwin) Irwin Araiza. Virginia was Stella's half sister, the daughter of Hattie and her first husband, Raymond Baldwin. After Hattie Redenbaugh was placed in a senior citizens' center in Topeka, Richard Araiza lived with Stella's brother Alvie "Junior" Irwin in the Clay Street home. Seematter recalled that her aunt was kind and personable and cared about the Araiza children, although she could be stern when the children were noisy and she thought they were disturbing Hattie. Stella had not lost what her prison counselors referred to as her "attitude." For example, according to Seematter, when Stella visited her mother in the senior citizens' center, she would bring Hattie's friends "stuff they weren't supposed to have," like chocolate or cigarettes. Confronted by staff, Stella told them, "Look, they lived their life and they can have what they want."

Stella was quirky and maintained unusual habits, including some that now appear to reflect her early years as a fugitive, according to family members. She paid for everything in cash that she kept in a money clip in her right pocket. She drove alarmingly fast. She kept important papers and other provisions in her car as if ready for a fast getaway. Stella remained a crack shot and sometimes practiced shooting by the Missouri River not far from her house.

Aunt Stella was quirky and stern but loving and generous, according to her great-nieces. Stella visited Topeka often, sometimes twice a week, to see her mother, disabled brother, half sister, and great-nieces. "She really loved her brother," Renee Araiza recalled. "Junior meant so much to her." During those years before Junior's and Hattie's deaths, Stella was the family caretaker, providing significant financial support and raising the question, now that the family knows of her past, of whether she may have recovered some of the money from the bank robberies after leaving prison. Somehow, despite working an hourly job as a store clerk, Stella was remarkably generous with her family. Over the years, she owned three houses, provided help with a down payment on Renee's home, gave away furniture, paid off hospital bills, and bought cars for Junior. Her generosity and limited means at least begs the question of whether Stella recovered some of the bank robbery money. It is at least possible that the note recovered by the FBI in which Ben claimed to have gambled away the majority of their bank robbery cash was a ruse like the letter claiming Ben had died was. The fact that Stella had, the day after the robbery, mailed $850 (the equivalent of more than $14,000 in 2015) to Topeka raises the question of whether there were other packages of cash that had been left with, mailed to, or otherwise recovered by Stella's mother. "We never heard them talk about their past, none of them, ever. Not Great Grandma [Hattie], or Junior or Stella," Renee Araiza said. When Araiza asked about her marriages, Stella closed the subject, saying, "We don't talk about our past."

One thing that Stella did talk about with Araiza was her work. She was proud of her work and often brought Renee to her workplace. In addition, Stella was a union activist, was a member of the Retail Clerks Local 782 in Kansas City, and had worked to unionize grocery checkers at several stores where she worked. "She told me that was the greatest accomplishment of her life," Araiza said. "The only thing she really talked to me a lot about was her job and getting the union going there."

In 1964, Stella filed legal paperwork making Gray the co-owner of the residence on Sycamore. In 1970, Gray gave up her stake in the property. Stella's pets, including show dogs and several dogs from a Missouri no-kill animal shelter, appear to have been her closest companions during the last twenty-five years of her life. Her love of animals was a source of amusement in the family. She kept a window air conditioner in only one room of the home, the living room, to keep that room cool for her dogs. When not in use, the air conditioner was covered by a large framed print. Renee Araiza recalled that Stella once stopped on Interstate Highway 70 on her way home to Kansas City from Topeka to pick up a dog wandering in the median. That dog lived out its life in her home. "She would talk to her animals like they were human beings," Renee said.

Stella took care of her parents as first stepfather Lester and then, later, Hattie's health failed, traveling between Kansas City and Topeka several times each week. In 1962, three years after Lester's death, Stella's mother and brother moved to Kansas City, apparently living from 1962 to 1963 in the house on East Terrace that Stella owned. They did not like living in the city and returned to Topeka after a short stay. Stella sold the East Terrace home in November 1963.

In her later years, Stella almost never spoke of Ben, whom she still referred to as Johnny, but she did confide a few details to a neighbor, telling her that Johnny had been the love of her life and showing her the photos from the 1938 Topeka Free Fair. Every New Year's Eve, according to the neighbor, Stella would stay home alone in her house and have a special meal, a shrimp salad, to commemorate a cherished memory from a New Year's Eve in 1938 or 1939 when she and "Johnny" were together. She told the neighbor, "This is what Johnny and I had." She did not admit her fugitive past, even to family, who had heard stories but were surprised to learn several years after Stella's death that their stern but loving aunt had been a public enemy. The revelations helped explain some of Stella's secretive or odd behavior, they said, such as her unwillingness to discuss her past and her reticence to appear in family pictures.

According to FBI reports, Stella briefly attended flight attendant and then beauty school and also trained in IBM computer punch card entry but eventually settled into a series of jobs as a drug store and supermarket checker in and around Raytown. She worked as a clerk at Seidlitz Paint and Varnish and at Katz Drug Store, both in Kansas City, for several years before shuttling through a series of supermarket checker jobs at various Justrite and Thriftway supermarkets. In 1967, she lost her job at Justrite Supermarket #5 in Raytown because her criminal record made it impossible to get a license to sell liquor.

In August 1967, mainly to allow her to get a liquor sales permit, Stella hired an attorney and applied for a presidential pardon. In her pardon application, she cited her youth at the time of the two bank robberies and asserted that she was coerced into participating by her much older husband. As it does with all executive clemency requests, the FBI began an investigation, turning up little of concern other than a couple of speeding tickets in the 1950s. Stella was arrested in 1953 for "check activities" but no charges were filed. In addition, the FBI suspected that during her time in Sioux City, she may have met one of the FBI's most wanted fugitives, David Daniel Keegan, who was wanted for murder, but Stella denied knowing him and agents abandoned that line of investigation. Affidavits from references included in the file included two from fellow supermarket checkers and one from

Stella Mae Irwin died in 1995 and was buried next to her brother, Junior, and next to her mother and stepfather in the Rochester Cemetery in north Topeka. (Photo by the author.)

a neighbor, who reported that Stella was "the quietest person in the neighborhood." One of her coworkers said Stella was "quiet and hard to get to know." In an interview with FBI agents, Stella said she sometimes went hunting and was a good shot. The FBI's report turned up nothing significant and, four years after she applied for clemency, on December 23, 1971, President Richard M. Nixon granted Stella Mae Irwin a full and unconditional pardon.

Stella's brother died in 1986. And in 1990, Hattie Redenbaugh died at the age of eighty-nine in a Topeka convalescent home. Stella had her mother buried next to Lester Redenbaugh, who died in 1959, in Rochester Cemetery in Topeka. After her mother's death, Stella's own health began to fail and she became more distant and disconnected from her extended family. "It was like she just gave up," Renee Araiza recalled.

"She had nothing anymore. Her mom passed away. Her brother passed away. My son and I spent a lot of time with her but something changed. She was still caring. She did a lot for me, but she just changed. She became a closeted person compared to what she was." In her will, Stella named her great-nephew and great-nieces but left them nothing "as they have been adequately taken care of while I was alive." Seematter was not upset about that. "I loved my aunt dearly," she said. "I didn't want any of her money, I loved her. Whatever she wanted to do was fine with me."

Suffering from emphysema, Stella became even more of a recluse after her mother's death, rarely leaving her home. A neighbor helped care for Stella as her health declined, spending many hours by her bedside talking. On September 10, 1995, Stella Mae Irwin died of complications from emphysema. She left $5,000 of her estate to the no-kill animal shelter where she had gotten her pets, M'Shoogy's Emergency Animal Rescue in Savannah, Missouri. Stella also left $5,000 to a Clay Street neighbor in Topeka. The remainder of her estate, about $77,000, was left to a neighbor in Raytown, a friend who had cared for her as her health declined.

Stella's remains were buried next to those of her brother, mother, and stepfather in Rochester Cemetery in north-central Topeka, an idyllic spot along Soldier Creek about a mile from the former site of the Ace Motor Court.

CONCLUSION

On Friday, August 17, 1945, a year before Stella emerged from prison and nine days before her twenty-third birthday, the FBI's authorized program on the ABC radio network, *This Is Your FBI*, aired an episode about bank robber Philip Houston and his young wife, Della. The script was based on the case of Ben and Stella Mae Dickson. Like Ben and Stella, Philip and Della were newlyweds who spent time at a lake resort, the fictional Illinois analogue of Lake Benton. Like Ben, Philip was a well-read young man from a good home. Philip and Della committed their crimes in Illinois instead of South Dakota, but the small-town banks are recognizable as stand-ins for banks in Brookings and Elkton. In the end, Philip, like Ben, was betrayed by a prison acquaintance. While Ben was shot in front of the Yankee System Hamburger Shop in St. Louis, Philip was killed by FBI agents in front of Joe's Hamburger Stand in Chicago. The stories are very similar, and yet the Ben character, Philip, is represented as almost comically evil, a nihilist spouting crackpot philosophy as justification for his crimes.

After the show's distinctive opening music and sponsor message, ("To your FBI, you look for national security, and to the Equitable Society for financial security") the narrator touted the program as providing a "public service." The August 17 episode opened with Philip Houston and his new bride, Della, walking along the shore at a lake resort. As the program joins them during their twilight walk, Philip has been preaching his twisted philosophy to Della and asks her to repeat what she has learned. The goal of life, Della says, is "to annihilate that which is weak, imperfect, ugly, and to build instead that which is strong, perfect, beautiful." Philip finishes the thought for her. "And that makes the act of annihilation itself beautiful." Not content to simply portray the Ben character as the adherent of a nihilist philosophy, the writer, Jerry Devine, offered a shocking demonstration of Philip's depravity. As they walk and talk, Della's dog, Skippy, bounds up to the couple and we hear the squeals of both as they play together on the sand. Unlike Ben and Stella, who loved dogs and even took a stranger's dog they found injured to a veterinarian and paid for its care, Philip sees Skippy's appearance as an opportunity to drive home his demented philosophical lesson. "You might as well test yourself right now," Philip says as Della continues playing with Skippy. "That kind of love is weakness. It rules the one who indulges it. You must overcome it now. Here, take this pistol."

"Why?" Della asks.

"The strong must be ready and able to inflict suffering or death upon any enemy of his strength," Philip says. "Shoot that dog, Della." Della refuses, and after accusing her of failing a test of obedience, Philip takes the pistol and shoots Skippy himself. After the gunshot, listeners hear the dog whimper and then go silent. From the myriad dramatic twists of the Dickson case that were available to him, producer-director Jerry Devine, who was hired by the FBI to supervise the program and write the original scripts, chose to twist real details like Ben's reading of Nietzsche and Stella's love of dogs into an opportunity to demonize him and portray her as his empty-headed and feckless moll. Other elements of the radio program came right out of the FBI's public relations template. Philip came from a good home with a "professor" father, proving, as the narrator confirms, that criminals can come from anywhere. The special agent who tracked the bank robbers (ironically, named Cameron like the only citizen witness of the Dickson shooting) used fingerprint science and analysis of automobile engine serial numbers, rather than paid informants, to narrow the hunt for Philip and Della. The scriptwriter even took a shot at one of Hoover's favorite foils, decrying the "lenient" parole system that allowed Philip to be released from the Kansas State Industrial Reformatory after serving just two years of a ten-year sentence. Presented as a "public service," *This Is Your FBI* was nothing more than public relations, fiction presented as fact.

The hero of the real story of Ben and Stella, inasmuch as it is possible for such a story to produce a hero, was Stella Mae Irwin, who "won" by surviving. Her life was an unending series of tragedies beginning with an abusive father and, at least until Lester Redenbaugh married Hattie, a distracted single mother. The horrific, scarring experience of rape at age fifteen was compounded by the invasive and dehumanizing treatment she received for a sexually transmitted disease. The pain of the situation was further exacerbated by the lack of counseling and by her shame when word leaked out about the rape and she found herself the subject of scorn among her schoolmates. Unable to face the shame, Stella ran away, right into the arms of the charismatic, handsome, and flawed Ben Dickson.

It is unclear whether or not Ben committed the cab robbery that initially sent him to prison. The circumstances of his trial, the long deliberation of the jury, and the claims of his respected father and brother suggest that Ben's arrest and conviction could well have been a mistake. What is clear is that Ben used his feelings of anger and frustration at what he perceived to be an injustice to explain away a series of robberies, starting in California and then moving to South Dakota, and probably elsewhere. Ben seems to have believed that the unfairness of being sent to the Kansas State Industrial Reformatory justified any acts necessary to set his life back in order. When he got out of Hutchinson as a teenager, Ben attempted to rob a Missouri bank with the help of one of his reformatory acquaintances. Convicted, rightly, of that crime, Ben spent six years in one of the most forbidding prisons in the United States, at Jefferson City, Missouri, and emerged even more convinced that he had been treated unfairly. In trouble again for punching the apparently unpleasant and possibly politically connected Irl Heidt, Ben fled Topeka. Ben, twenty-six, then ensnared his fifteen-year-old bride in his criminal lifestyle as well, convincing her that the real or perceived miscarriage of justice that led him to a life of crime somehow excused further crimes so long as he expressed a goal of starting over and doing good. Ben thus involved Stella, an impressionable and romantic teenager, in his bank robbery schemes. Stella naively followed her charismatic husband into the banks they robbed, obeyed his orders during the kidnapping of three men in Michigan, and, when he told her to, fired the only two shots the duo fired during their time together, disabling or discouraging two pursuing Michigan State Police officers.

The Dicksons' story does not reflect well on the professionalism of 1930s local law enforcement or on the integrity of local and federal justice systems of the time. Topeka Police officers and Shawnee County sheriff's deputies seem to have happily mistaken the small-time criminal Ben Dickson for a deranged and murderous outlaw like Clyde Barrow of Bonnie and Clyde. The Topeka officers were overzealous when they fired forty-eight shots at Dickson, endangering Stella, Elizabeth Musick, potentially other bystanders, and each other, at the Ace Motor Court in November 1938. At the time, Dickson was charged only with punching a DMV official. No doubt the shoot-first mentality displayed by the police that day helped convince Stella that Ben and, thereafter, both of them were being persecuted by out-of-control law enforcement officers. No doubt their feelings of persecution only increased when two Michigan State Police officers who encountered the Dicksons near Leonidas, Michigan, shot first and asked questions later. Ben Dickson's death on the street in St. Louis, shot by one of four FBI agents on the scene as he tried to run away, was the logical conclusion to that progression of overzealous police tactics.

In its investigation of the case, the FBI demonstrated its remarkable and innovative ability to sift through a mountain of information from various sources to piece together a case. The Bureau's meticulous detective work, chasing down every miniscule detail, was remarkable, a credit to the professionalized law enforcement agency Hoover had created. Bureau agents even managed to trace the origin of the roofing nails tossed from the car by Stella at the corner of Sixth Street and Medary Avenue after the Brookings robbery, though that detail proved irrelevant to the case. As a result of thousands of hours of meticulous investigation with no detail too small to pursue, the Bureau managed to locate an informant who in turn led them directly to Ben Dickson outside the Yankee System Hamburger Shop in St. Louis. The detective work displayed by FBI agents in seeking the Dicksons, who after all had fallen off the map in late 1938, can only be judged as first-rate. As a result of that work, agents found themselves on the same sidewalk in St. Louis with Ben on April 6, 1939. At that point, though, the agents' actions also confirmed the judgments of critics who said the FBI was reckless and too frequently acted as judge and jury, killing their designated public enemies first and asking questions later. Agent John Bush, who no doubt saw Ben turn and attempt to flee, nevertheless fired the two shots that hit the fugitive in the side and back, killing him. Meanwhile, three other agents stood by and withheld their fire, indicating that they did not feel threatened by Ben's actions.

In the aftermath of the shooting, FBI officials demonstrated that they valued public relations and the protection of the Bureau's reputation over any legitimate quest for truth and justice. The SAC in St. Louis and the chief of the Bureau's Investigative Division, a future federal judge, concocted a story that matched the kind of heroic image of the FBI that Hoover demanded. When their newly authored version of events was threatened by a legal proceeding, a St. Louis County coroner's inquest, FBI officials rigged the hearing and attempted to silence the only credible witness, waitress Gloria Cameron.

The St. Louis FBI agents further bungled the case by failing to account for Public Enemy No. 2, Stella, who saw her husband dying on the sidewalk as she sped away from the scene while the agents, perhaps stunned by their colleagues' violent response to Ben's efforts to escape, watched her drive away. Portrayed by the Bureau and its friends in the news media as a ruthless and violent gun moll, Stella was in reality an emotionally devastated teen who had been living the stressful life of a fugitive for months and had just witnessed the violent death of her husband. Stella simply wanted to get home to her mother. Because of the FBI's mistakes, one that led to the unnecessary killing of Ben and the other that let Stella escape the scene, a moment that could have been a triumph of FBI investigative prowess had to be salvaged after the fact by a version of events created by a local SAC and a future federal judge in Washington, a story of the shooting that is largely fictional.

A rational, progressive criminal justice system would have recognized Stella Mae Dickson for what she was: a naive minor who turned to crime only at the encouragement of, or perhaps coerced by, her much older husband. George Philips, the US attorney in South Dakota, saw Stella up close and came to the conclusion that she deserved probation. The reporters who saw her in the Kansas City federal building and in a South Dakota courthouse recognized Stella as a child. Philips was unsure how to proceed and, in a letter to the attorney general, admitted that probation would likely be the appropriate punishment for a minor like Stella. In yet another tragic turn for Stella, FBI Director J. Edgar Hoover, isolated behind his desk thousands of miles away in Washington, where it was easy to render judgment on a "vicious gun moll" like Stella, maneuvered to force prison time on the sixteen-year-old. Hoover pressured Attorney General Frank Murphy, who, in what appears to have been an unethical, ex parte communication, had one of his assistants send a telegram to the trial judge in Deadwood, South Dakota, urging that Stella be sentenced to the federal women's reformatory at Alderson, West Virginia.

Stella, who was fifteen at the time of the Elkton robbery and sixteen when she stood by in the lobby while Ben robbed the Northwest Security National Bank in Brookings, was sentenced to two concurrent ten-year terms in Alderson for her tag-along role in the crimes. In both instances, she held a gun and stood nearby as Dickson robbed the banks. In at least one instance, her entry into the bank was an accident caused by her own anxiety for her husband's well-being when he did not return to the car quickly enough. There is no evidence that Stella initiated any of their crimes or that she would have become a criminal had she been left on her own. The coverture defense was relatively common in the 1920s and 1930s, and if anyone ever deserved consideration under that principle, Stella Mae Dickson did. Instead she was shipped off to Alderson.

In prison, "counselors" inexplicably seemed unable to understand why Stella, abused child, teenage rape victim, widow, and inmate, might be carrying such anger about the way her life turned out. As a result, Stella's time in the reformatory was marked by lengthy stretches in solitary confinement, bouts of severe anxiety, and chronic difficulty maintaining a healthy weight. When she was discharged, in 1946, she finally made it home to her mother. But it would not be long before yet another tragedy, domestic abuse by a much older husband, fell upon her during an ill-advised marriage. It is easy to imagine that Stella, an ex-convict with no high school degree, married Ralph Daugherty in search of the kind of stability that she had never found at home or with Ben. Instead, she got only more turmoil and pain. Stella's later years were spent in seclusion in her Kansas City home, working service jobs but managing to put together something of a normal life with her beloved dogs as companions. The only clear victory of any kind during her tragedy-marred life came in 1971, when at last someone looked dispassionately at the circumstances of her 1939 sentence and she was granted a presidential pardon by Richard Nixon for the crimes she participated in as a teenager. That pardon did not, of course, alter the nature of her reality or fix the tragedies of her life, but it must have felt like a victory of a sort for her. Nevertheless, she remained a recluse from everyone but her family until her death from emphysema at age seventy-three in 1995.

Some members of the Dickson family and others have portrayed Ben as a victim. In an April 8, 1939, editorial, the *Topeka Daily Capital*

Stella Mae Irwin, portrait taken in the late 1940s or early 1950s. (Photo courtesy of Gloria Seematter, from the Araiza family collection.)

declared, "It is a serious indictment of the American penal system that few persons confined for infractions of law ever again become adjusted to society's rules." There is no doubt that a more rehabilitative criminal justice system combined with a more rational police response to his early missteps might have changed Ben's life. He was smart and handsome and the product of a loving and stable family, notably of a father who never gave up on him and tried repeatedly to help him salvage a normal life. Notably, Ben's brother Darwin was a product of the same home and lived a long, productive life, obtaining a good education, working with skill and dignity at a railroad job for decades, and raising a family of his own. The preacher's words at Ben's funeral about a good boy gone wrong who had been treated unjustly contained a nugget of truth. It appears possible that Ben did not commit the cab robbery that sent him to the Hutchinson Reformatory as a teenager. Even the FBI did not trust Topeka Police accounts of the cab robbery. It took nearly three days for a jury in what should have been a simple case to convict Dickson. Later, it appears possible that Topeka Police were responding to political pressure when they charged Ben with a serious felony after his fight with Irl Heidt. Faced with injustice, Ben chose the wrong path in his often frustrated efforts to rehabilitate his life. Rather than opting for the difficult and time-consuming choice of working his way back into the community's good graces, he sought a quick payday to set him up for success. That choice led to a collision with FBI Director J. Edgar Hoover, who could not have dreamed of a better public relations story to peddle to the press than the quest to capture or kill another Bonnie and Clyde–style outlaw couple. Ben was the handsome son of a respected family. Stella was a pretty blonde who had been photographed holding two guns and thus could easily be forced into the mold of the 1930s gun moll. Unfortunately, Ben did not bring Hoover's wrath upon himself alone. He dragged his young wife into his crime spree. He brought shame upon the house of his parents, respected Topeka residents who never stopped trying to help him.

If the family's claims about Dickson's initial innocence are true, then injustice bookended Ben's adult life. He may not have been guilty of the cab robbery, and the last act of his life was clearly an injustice as he was shot on the street by an overzealous FBI agent. Guilty of bank robbery and kidnapping or not, being shot by an FBI agent while running away is not the due process Americans are guaranteed. In between those bookends of injustice, though, one could say that Ben got the life he made for himself. At a time when the FBI was becoming a national icon, Ben cast himself in Hoover's public relations tales. Ben may have been a good boy gone wrong, as his family suggested, but through his actions, he brought shame upon his immediate family and inflicted further tragedy on his young wife, Stella, whose adult life began on Halloween 1937 with an attack that left her deeply wounded and in need of stability and understanding. Instead, she was dragged into the vagabond life of a fugitive. As *Topeka Daily Capital* editors noted two days after Ben Dickson's death: "While it is difficult to picture Ben Dickson as a bad boy, the evidence was against him. His family deserves the community's sympathy, and has it." One might rightly edit that sentence this way: Ben's family, most of all his young wife Stella, deserves the community's sympathy.

NOTES

INTRODUCTION

1. FBI Interesting Case Memorandum 7-2561, May 1939, 1.

2. Henry Bartlett, "The Crimson Trail of Public Enemies One and Two," *True*, May 1939, 5.

3. For a full discussion of the Bureau's public relations efforts, see Matthew Cecil, *Hoover's FBI and the Fourth Estate: The Campaign to Control the Press and the Bureau's Image* (Lawrence: University Press of Kansas, 2014).

CHAPTER 1. STELLA

1. Descriptions of Stella's capture from FBI files including V. P. Keay, Investigative Summary, Stella Mae Dickson, April 22, 1939, FBI 29-100-651, 6.

2. Stella Mae Dickson was born Estelle Mae Irwin. She was apparently adopted by her stepfather and became Estelle (Stella) Mae Redenbaugh. After her husband's death and a later divorce, she became known as Stella Mae Irwin.

3. Descriptions of Stella's early life come from the FBI's investigation for her presidential pardon (FBI file 73-15944) and her Bureau of Prisons file.

4. Chapmon Fletcher, FBI Investigative Summary, September 5, 1939, Bureau of Prisons file, Stella Mae Dickson.

5. T. Benedek, "History of the Medical Treatment of Gonorrhea," retrieved from http://www.antimicrobe.org/h04c.files/history/Gonorrhea.asp, accessed March 30, 2016.

CHAPTER 2. BEN

1. "Ben" will be used throughout this narrative, rather than "Benny" or "Bennie," because that is how Darwin Dickson referred to his brother.

2. James Darwin Dickson of Colony, Kansas, was telephonically interviewed by the author twice in the summer of 1995.

3. Shawnee County District Court, State of Kansas v. Bennie Dickson, Journal Entry for Case No. 12465, June 25 to July 1, 1929.

4. Richard Dickson was interviewed in Wichita, Kansas, in November 2015.

5. Waldon O. Peterson, "A Look Back at the Lake Benton Summer Resort," *Lincoln County* (Minn.) *Valley Journal*, July 17, 1996, 9–12.

6. Richard Araiza, Renee Araiza, and Gloria Seematter were interviewed in Topeka, Kansas, December 2015.

CHAPTER 3. J. EDGAR HOOVER'S FBI

1. For a brief overview of the history of the FBI, see Athan Theoharis, Tony G. Poveda, Susan Rosenfeld, and Richard Gid Powers, eds., *The FBI: A Comprehensive Reference Guide* (New York: Oryx Press, 2000), 2–43.

2. Kenneth O'Reilly, "A New Deal for the FBI: The Roosevelt Administration, Crime Control, and National Security," *Journal of American History* 69, no. 3 (December 1982): 638–658.

3. For a comprehensive review of Hoover's life and legacy, see Athan Theoharis and John Stuart Cox, *The Boss: J. Edgar Hoover and the Great American Inquisition* (Philadelphia: Temple University Press, 1988).

CHAPTER 4. TIME LOCK BANDITS

1. The Elkton robbery details are included in multiple FBI files but are summarized in W. H. Heywood, Investigative Summary, September 10, 1938, FBI 29-100-589.

2. Amy Dunkle, *The College on the Hill: A Sense of South Dakota State University History* (Brookings: SDSU Alumni Association, 2003).

3. The Brookings robbery details are included in multiple FBI files but are summarized in R. L. Nalls, Investigative Summary, November 10, 1938, FBI 29-100-656.

4. "Man, Girl Rob Brookings Bank of $15,000," *Sioux Falls Daily Argus Leader*, October 31, 1938, 1.

5. Charles "Tim" Monahan, interviewed by the author, October 14, 1995.

CHAPTER 5. PUBLIC ENEMIES

1. Details of the Michigan kidnapping in several FBI files, summarized in F. G. Johnstone, Summary Memorandum, April 28, 1939, FBI 29-100-654.

CHAPTER 6. ST. LOUIS

1. The events leading up to Ben Dickson's shooting are summarized in Gerald B. Norris, Summary Memorandum, April 3, 1939, FBI 7-2561-559.

2. The key sources of information about Dickson's shooting are Gerald B. Norris, Personal and Confidential Letter to J. Edgar Hoover, April 7, 1939, FBI 7-2561-604X; Edward A. Tamm, memorandum to J. Edgar Hoover, April 9, 1939, FBI 7-2461-604; Edward A. Tamm, memorandum to J. Edgar Hoover, April 9, 1939, FBI 7-2461-729; Gerald B. Norris, Investigative Summary, April 9, 1939, FBI 7-2461-5.

3. Louis Cochran, *FBI Man: A Personal History* (New York: Duell, Sloan, and Pierce, 1966), 187.

CHAPTER 7. HOME TO MOTHER

1. "Stella Mae Dickson Tells How Her Desperado Husband Was Shot to Death by G-Men," *Sioux Falls Daily Argus Leader*, April 11, 1939, 8.

2. Stella's post-prison life is documented in an FBI investigation conducted as a result of her request for a presidential pardon, FBI 73-15944.

3. Stella's neighbor, Sharon Michael, was interviewed by the author twice in 1999. Repeated attempts to contact her in 2015 were unsuccessful.

A NOTE ON SOURCES

This book is based primarily on FBI files that included such vital primary sources as Stella Mae Dickson's two written confessions, the transcript of the St. Louis County coroner's inquest into Ben Dickson's shooting, the many detailed FBI Investigative Summaries from across the country, and hundreds of internal Bureau memoranda related to the case. Stella Mae Irwin's application for clemency prompted another FBI investigation and a file of documents that yielded many clues about her post-prison life. In addition to those documents, court documents from Shawnee County, Kansas, and federal court documents from South Dakota were consulted. Stella Mae Dickson's Bureau of Prisons file from her stay in Alderson, West Virginia, and Seagoville, Texas, included detailed reports on progress-report interviews that provided tremendous detail about her mental condition following the multiple ordeals she endured. Two 1999 interviews with Stella Mae Irwin's longtime neighbor and friend, Sharon Michael, were helpful in filling in the details of her later life. Two interviews with Ben Dickson's brother Darwin, both of them from the mid-1990s, provided background on Ben's childhood and on the family's feelings about their brother and son. Interviews with Ben's relative Richard Dickson and with Stella's relatives Gloria Seematter, Renee Araiza, and Richard Araiza provided additional insight into the families.

While an enormous cache of documentary information was available for this study, photographs proved much more difficult to find. Photographs of buildings and the like are relatively easy to find in state historical societies and university special collections. The availability of historical news photographs depends entirely on whether individual newspaper companies have bothered to maintain their archives. The tendency of many newspapers to destroy (or in some cases, somehow lose) their photographic archives is, to this historian, alarming and unforgiveable. Another disturbing development in the availability of historical photographs is the fact that many extraordinary collections have been sold to for-profit companies that have simply chosen not to digitize older photographs or offer them for publication. Dozens of photographs from the Dickson case no doubt exist in for-profit archives but are simply unavailable to scholars.

Thank goodness, then, that surviving members of the two families made their collections of photographs available for this volume. Richard Dickson generously allowed the author to rummage through a trunk full of family photos left to him by his father, Ben's brother Darwin Dickson. And Gloria Seematter and Renee Araiza provided access to the photos that their Great-Aunt Stella left to them.

SELECTED BIBLIOGRAPHY

FBI FILES

John Bush (67-20851), Louis Cochran (FBI 67-43234), Bennie [*sic*] Dickson (FBI 7-2561), Ben Dickson (FBI 29-100, via National Archives and Records Administration), Stella Mae Irwin (FBI 73-15944), Louis B. Nichols (FBI 67-39021), Gerald B. Norris (67-4040), John B. Oakes (FBI 94-8-51), Edward A. Tamm (FBI 67-15585), Clyde Tolson (67-9524)

BOOKS/ARTICLES

Cecil, Matthew. *Hoover's FBI and the Fourth Estate: The Campaign to Control the Press and the Bureau's Image.* Lawrence: University Press of Kansas, 2014.

O'Reilly, Kenneth. "A New Deal for the FBI: The Roosevelt Administration, Crime Control, and National Security." *Journal of American History* 69, no. 3 (December 1982): 638–658.

Powers, Richard Gid. *G-Men: Hoover's FBI in American Popular Culture.* Carbondale and Edwardsville: Southern Illinois University Press, 1983.

Theoharis, Athan, and John Stuart Cox. *The Boss: J. Edgar Hoover and the Great American Inquisition.* Philadelphia: Temple University Press, 1988.

Theoharis, Athan, Tony G. Poveda, Susan Rosenfeld, and Richard Gid Powers, eds. *The FBI: A Comprehensive Reference Guide.* New York: Oryx Press, 2000.

NEWSPAPERS

Brookings (S.D.) *County Press*
Brookings (S.D.) *Daily Register*
Elkton (S.D.) *Record*
Kansas City (Mo.) *Journal*
Kansas City (Mo.) *Star*
Kansas City (Mo.) *Times*
Sioux Falls (S.D.) *Daily Argus Leader*
St. Louis (Mo.) *Globe-Democrat*
St. Louis (Mo.) *Post-Dispatch*
Topeka (Kan.) *Daily Capital*
Topeka (Kan.) *State Journal*

INDEX

and criminal justice system, 167

dangerousness of, 3, 7, 8, 28, 35–36, 53, 94, 96, 99, 125, 132

death of, 1, 7, 17, 20, 30, 116, 117, 118, 121, 127, 129, 131, 136, 162, 168

and death of brother Spencer, 46

as desperate for money, 51, 85

and Dickson family, 23, 25, 29, 101, 165, 167, 168

and difficulties finding work due to criminal record, 51, 52

and Elkton, SD, robbery, 63–69, 99, 165

and encounter with Sheriff Wayne Horning and his deputies, 35–36

and false allegations of murder, 125

and fate of money from Brookings robbery, 85–86

father of, 138

FBI file of, 6–7, 28, 111

and FBI's portrayal of as a vicious killer, 128, 129

and FBI's radio show program, 159–161

and federal counts of kidnapping, 99, 102

and feelings as justification for robberies with Stella, 43, 50–51, 161

and fight with Edward "Irl" Heidt, 39–40, 49, 50, 88, 89, 94, 99, 125, 162, 167

as a fugitive, 7, 8, 41, 47–48, 49, 52, 88, 91–92, 93, 96, 100

as a fugitive from the law, 101, 102–105, 106, 107, 141–142

funeral of, 142–143

and gambling, 40, 66, 86, 154

grave of, 143 (fig.)

and guilt in cab robbery incident, 161, 167–168

and hometown of Topeka, KS, 23–25, 73, 87

and hostage Louis Karr, 98

and hostages Minnis and Metty, 96–98

as an immoral nihilist, 3, 159

and influence of his father in his education, 43, 105

and influence on Stella Mae, 34, 51, 162

injuries of, 92, 94, 100, 102, 103, 104

as inmate of the Missouri State Penitentiary, 37–38, 38 (fig.)

and involvement with criminal justice system as a teen, 28, 31–34

and Kansas State Industrial Reformatory, 31, 33, 34, 36, 101, 161, 167

and kidnapping, 7, 96–99, 136, 142, 167

and letter from Stella to her mother as a ruse, 102–104

and letters to Stella from CA, 42–43

and life in New Orleans, 104–105, 108–110

and location of in St. Louis, 106

and love of dogs, 160

and marriage to Stella, 138

and marriage to Stella in Pipestone, MN, 51, 63

as mastermind of robberies, 136, 162

media accounts of shooting of, 128–129

and meeting Stella at a roller-skating rink, 39

and meeting with Naomi at FBI stake-out location, 115, 123

and meeting with Stella in CA, 16–17

and money robbed from Elkton, SD, bank, 69, 71

and Naomi in St. Louis, 111–112

and obtaining multiple cars, 88, 98, 100, 105

other girlfriends of, 16, 40, 41, 44

personal items in suitcases of, 92–93

and pictures of in the media, 101

and planning bank robberies, 136

and plans to rob bank in Brookings, SD, 73, 92

poetry and, 1, 43, 105, 109, 133

prison years of, 37–38, 51–52

and personal items of the Dicksons, 105, 106, 109

and photo of Stella with a pistol and rifle, 49

and portrayal of Ben and Stella as immoral criminals, 7, 132

press releases of, 1, 3, 28, 49, 60, 94, 100, 101, 104, 107, 110, 126, 137

and prison inmate friend of Ben who turned him in, 38, 99, 110

and promotion of agency's utility, 53, 60

and public enemies, 99, 102, 107, 123, 125–126, 128, 163–164

and public relations, 2–4, 7–8, 28, 53, 59–61, 99, 101–102, 105–106, 160–161, 163, 167, 168

public's view of, 60–61, 119

and public version of shooting of Ben Dickson, 116, 119, 120–121, 126, 163, 164

and radio show program, 126, 159–161

and recovery of Ben Dickson's guns and personal effects, 41, 49, 105

and robbery money Stella mailed to herself, 134

secret files of, 6

and self-defense shootings, 128

self-promotion campaigns of, 2, 4, 53, 59–60

and selling of the Dickson story, 2, 49, 126

and shooting of Ben Dickson, 1, 20, 115–129, 162, 163–164, 167

and "shootout" at the Ace Motor Court, 94, 102, 125

and sightings of the Dicksons, 101, 103

and Special Agent in Charge Edward P. Guinane, 21–22, 101, 106

and Special Agent in Charge Gerald B. Norris, 112, 113 (fig.), 114, 115, 116, 117–124, 126, 129, 132

and Special Agent in Charge Werner Hanni, 69, 133

and Special Agent L. B. Reed, 134, 135

and Special Agents R. H. Hallenberg, F. G. McGeary, and H. O. Hawkins, 21

and spying on dissenting Americans, 60

and stakeout of Yankee System Hamburger Shop, 113–115

and Stella as a gun moll, 48–49, 64, 134

and Stella Mae Dickson as a fugitive, 91–92

and Stella Mae Dickson's escape in St. Louis, 129–130

and Stella's account of Ben hiding money, 69, 71

and Stella's account of driving with hostages Metty and Minnis, 97–98

and Stella's account of Topeka Police at Ace Motor Court, 90, 91

and Stella's confession without an attorney present, 133–134

and Stella talking about plans to rob Elkton bank, 50, 65

and St. Louis agents Cochran, Pratt, and Bush, 114, 115, 116, 118, 120–122, 124, 125

and stores of historical evidence, 5, 6, 60

success of, 4, 5

and testimony of Norris regarding Dickson's shooting, 123–125

and tip from Vernon Jackson, 76–77, 85

and use of force against fugitives, 127

and use of guns, 55, 56, 116–117, 120–125, 128

and use of science, 3, 6, 60

and wanted posters for Ben and Stella, 99, 100, 101, 104

and warrants, 56

and wiretapping of telephones, 112, 129

and "woman in black," 123, 124, 125, 129, 136

and the "woman in red," 19, 115, 129

during World War II, 53, 60

See also Bureau of Investigation; G-Men; Hoover, J. Edgar; Nichols, Louis B.; public enemies; This Is Your FBI